FLOWERS AND FRUIT

COLETTE

FLOWERS AND FRUIT

Edited by Robert Phelps

Translated by Matthew Ward

Farrar Straus Giroux, New York

Library of Congress Cataloging in Publication Data

Colette, 1873–1954.
Flowers and fruit.
Contents: Translator's note—For an herbarium—
A nosegay—[etc.]
1. Colette, 1873–1954—Translations, English.
2. Flowers—Addresses, essays, lectures.
3. Gardening—Addresses, essays, lectures.
I. Phelps, Robert.   II. Title.
PQ2605.O28A285   1986   844'.912   85–16271

CONTENTS

EDITOR'S NOTE

Even in her native France, Colette remains best known as a novelist, as the author of *Chéri*, *The Vagabond*, *Gigi*, and a hundred other tales. Yet more than half of her published writing is nonfiction—vivid personal essays, intimate soliloquies, portraits of the human, animal, and vegetable kingdoms—and in every case, no matter what the nominal subject may be, the real subject is Colette herself, raptly, reverently watching some part of the created world enact its living drama.

Flowers and Fruit is a selection of portraits of the vegetable kingdom—gardens and orchards, roses and wistaria, oranges and medicinal herbs, orchids and poppies and anemones, tulips and hyacinths and gardenias. Most were written in the last decades of Colette's working life, when she was crippled with arthritis and had to spend most of her time on the divan bed she called her "raft."

The first group, "For an Herbarium," was begun when an imaginative Swiss publisher made Colette an enticing offer. "Once or twice a week," he proposed, "I'll send you some flowers. When one of the bouquets inspires you, you'll sketch its portrait, and after a year or so, we'll make a little book."

"A Nosegay" draws on material which remained unpublished in book form during Colette's lifetime. It includes the earliest piece reprinted here ("Flower Shows," from a weekly column she wrote in 1924), as well as "The Life and Death of the Phyllocactus," one of the last and tenderest she wrote.

Finally, "Flora and Pomona" was put together by Colette herself, and appeared in a deluxe edition in the darkest days of Nazi-occupied Paris. The money it earned helped to keep the coal bin at 9, rue de Beaujolais well filled and paid the black-market prices for rabbit and cheese and chicken and other comestibles otherwise unavailable, even to much-loved novelists living in the Palais-Royal.

"My poetry is earthbound," Colette once said. In these thirty-eight portraits, this is literally true.

—Robert Phelps

Editor's Note

TRANSLATOR'S NOTE

Nothing is more exacting than love and no one's love was more exacting than Colette's. Of every sentence that set out to describe something she cherished—the memory of a face, a place, an animal, a flower—much was demanded. Driven by this love, her writings on flowers and fruit rank among the most exalted, the most ecstatically pagan rhapsodies to the plant kingdom ever composed. In a marriage of precise, botanical nomenclature and poetic inspiration, Colette achieved the full flowering of the classical style for which she is so justly celebrated.

"Pleasure," writes Colette, "derives from what we have forgotten." In the midst of war, scarcity, and confinement, the aging Colette set out to remember. In the literature of evocation naming is all-important, tantamount to possession. Most have perhaps forgotten that the word "pagan" shares roots with the word "peasant" and means, in its most ancient acceptation, of or from the earth. Here the pagan spirit in Colette summons forth a vocabulary of staggering breadth and names in a spirit of Latinity. No other modern French writer, with the exception perhaps of Valéry, sounds the Latin value of the French language more purely. Certainly none sounds it so instinctively. Anyone who would translate these late writings into English soon must resign himself to the greater distance from English to Latin than from French to Latin, and concede much ground. Colette uses this instinctive Latinity in the service of a diction whose purity is Racinian. Mauriac was not the only one to note the affinity between the two. Colette can write *"la fleur"* and invest it with all the ideational abstraction of Racine and in the next breath give us a list of flowers with all the reality of Shakespeare. The movement from the one to the other was a mere exhalation, an inhalation.

Many find Colette "difficult." But I have come to believe that Colette herself was innocent of a certain type of difficulty. Lucie Delarue-Mardrus once complained in a letter to Colette that she used too many obscure words. To this Colette replied, "But, my dear, where I come from, we were already calling cammock by its name when I was a child. Cammock or rest-harrow. It isn't my fault." It would be easy to regard her response as pedantic or didactic but, just as she admired Redouté for his botanical learning because "it helped him to establish a style, to heighten a floral attitude with authority," she, too, was trying to establish a kind of authority, not over cammock or roses, but over memory. Relentless memory and uncompromising love, I think, are the worst she can be faulted with. Countless times I was sent to *Littré* or *Robert* in search of the particular way in which Colette was using a word only to find that it was its archaic, its Latin, its original, its forgotten meaning she intended, which was necessary in her attempt to repossess, to reanimate, to reinhabit the word. Exaction came naturally to Colette.

I believe it was Mme de Staël who identified style with *le naturel*, by which she did not mean nature but what in a writer's work is most authentic. In these writings Colette achieves what she says Redouté achieved, "the lyricism of exactitude." Translating them often seemed like an attempt to turn a botany text into poetry. Any translation, with its forced enlargements and reductions, can be considered a hybrid of sorts, but in this instance the comparison seems particularly apt. As with any hybrid flower, the first quality to be lost is fragrance, perfume, the flood of nuance which in the French original is at times as overwhelming as a room too full of lilies. However, unlike Colette's and Redouté's, the translator's own scrupulousness has not everywhere lost its documentary modesty. And though at times these renderings may seem the faded and scentless remnants of flowers that once flourished in their native soil, it is not for lack of love.

I would like to thank my two editors at Farrar, Straus and Giroux, Nancy Miller, who first asked me to translate these pieces, and Carol McKeown, whose patience and care have been everywhere admirable, and, of course, Robert Phelps. Lynn Warshow did yeoman's service copy editing manuscript and galleys and I thank her. To my fellow translator and dear friend Irene Ilton I am deeply indebted. The text benefited immeasurably from the attention given it by the poet Jean Jacobson, without whom it would never have been completed. Mrs. Lothian Lynas of the New York Botanical Gardens, Katia Lutz, Françoise Geoffrion, and Ruth Jacobson all made significant contributions. And, as ever, my deep gratitude and respect to Richard Howard, who is always there when I need him.

—Matthew Ward

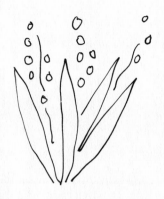

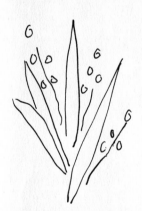

FOR AN HERBARIUM

ROSE

It is not the first of the season, by any means. Before it, our chilly climate rouses the violet, the Easter primrose, the daffodil, the potentilla with flowers like the wild strawberry's, hepatica, yellow iris along the water's edge . . . Are we energumens, or the tropics, or mad Provence, to hope that here where we live, January will bring the bloom to the Rose?

But I see that we are sufficiently intoxicated by it for me to grant its name a capital R; all the more so because the last war priced it like gold, just as it did calf's liver and pineapples. "How much is that rose?" a lady would ask timidly, poking her head into the flower shop. Before there was time for an answer, she would put her hands over her ears and say, "No, don't tell me!" and beat a hasty retreat. It was just that the shop was resplendent with those roses that have lips, cheeks, breasts, navels, flesh glistening with an indescribable frost; roses that travel by air, stand erect on the end of a disdainful stem, and smell of peaches, tea, and even of roses . . . Unattainable roses. Rose, wherein are your former lovers satisfied? Like all lovers aged or dethroned, they content themselves with singing your praises. They gaze at you longingly, through the shop window. They sigh, they can describe you in covetous detail, they talk about your shape, about the tight whorl your hybrid nature requires. I think that, like me, they miss the blessed days of your imperfection. We would buy you as God had made you, a little bitten here, a little rusted there, and it was left to us to trim you, unless we preferred you rusted and bitten, with a rose chafer hidden in the conch of your ear. You had too many leaves, spots like a radish's, a little snail along your stem, and as many thorns as a touchy maiden. Now the florist picks and plucks at you with the tweezers, and tears your ladybugs and your ants from you, and two or three outer rows of petals as well.

Lovely with neither blight nor blemish, I love you best at Bagatelle or L'Hay. I will come to see you one warm, fresh June day, when you are plundered by whirlwinds and make us believe that you can still give of yourself unstintingly. There, pointlessly, I will read your names, which, thank God, I will forget forthwith. What do I care about your social standing, decorated as you are with the names of this or that old general or big industrialist or some Madame Robinet or other. President

For an Herbarium

Herriot passes muster because he has the bearing—and the skill—of a true gardener. But you are better baptized in my religion, Rose, you whom in secret I name Scarlet Sin, Apricot Plum, Snow, Fairy, Black Beauty; you who so gloriously bear the homage of a truly pagan name, Thigh-of-the-trembling-nymph.

Below my window, among the puddles of water, the bathing pigeons, the lawns trimmed à la Bressant, the althea clipped into spheres, and the canna, we have old-fashioned, floriferous rosebushes that have survived both war and frost. Never have they failed to flower, and to flower again, and yet again before November. They disarm even the children of the first arrondissement, well known for their ferocity. By an odd bit of grafting, one of the smallest bushes bears blooms that are half yellow, half red. Another, a sulphur rose, doubled and redoubled, loads its stake with a richness . . . A richness . . . How can I tell you? . . . These roses in the Palais-Royal, these prodigious old rosebushes . . . in what words can I rush off a description to the Parc des Eaux-Vives in Geneva, which I have gazed upon in its full glory, that will make the Swiss rose garden green with envy! Long-stemmed roses, their buds closed like eggs, then open all of a sudden, roses in the heart of Paris awakened by the rainbow trapped in a spray of water, I search for something to compare you with; in what Eden could I gather flowers that are your equal . . . I think I know. You are nearly as beautiful as the cascade of roses that spills over a gatekeeper's tiny yard, covers a gardener's cottage, or lattices the wall of a country inn, here, there, wherever they show, for us to marvel at, the possibilities in the coming together of June, chance, and a beautiful day, the solitude of a young girl, the hand of a dreamy old man and his kindly pruning shears . . .

For an Herbarium

LILY

Lys! et l'un de vous tous pour l'ingénuité.

What I have to say about it I say by way of ruse and rote. In the presence of a lily, or several lilies, a voice from the group is always raised to quote Mallarmé with literary fervor:

Lys! et l'un de vous tous pour l'ingénuité.

Since I am alone today, and since my daughter came and left me a lily, I did not fail to exclaim to myself, "*Lys! et l'un de vous tous . . .*" But my heart wasn't in it. Nor my intonation. I was embarrassed as I am when I try on a friend's feathered hat or her earrings and I see consternation written on the faces around me. I would like to give it another try, beginning a line higher to work up to it:

Droit et seul, sous un flot antique de lumière,
*Lys! et l'un de vous tous pour l'ingénuité.**

But let's not dwell on this any longer. It requires greater art and greater love than mine—Henri Mondor, forgive me!—to do justice to a poem whose glory was assured by the music of Claude Debussy.

I date from far enough back for certain details from my antiquity to amuse me. When *L'Aprés-Midi d'un faune* was surrounded on the one side by denunciation and on the other by spirited enthusiasm, I had already seen the passing of the time when Jules Lemaître—in the *Revue Bleue,* I believe—"explained" (*sic*) to the masses the little poem by Verlaine:

L'espoir luit comme un brin de paille dans l'étable† . . .

I have not forgotten that, on so unexpected a task of mediation, the future author of *La Massière* hazarded more wit than understanding, and more ridicule than wit. Did he bring the same hand, with the same heaviness, to bear on Mallarmé? Talk of it never reached me. Around the pagan triad I perceived only a buzzing of bees, the discreet scandal surrounding *L'Aprés-Midi d'un faune,* when the commentators emphasized the fact that the sensual diversions of the cloven-hoofed faun and the two nymphs composed an uneven grouping.

I knew nothing of the poet as a man. His pleasant, distinguished face, with its goatee, has passed quite near

---

* Lone and erect, beneath light's primal flood,
   A lily! and pure as any one of you.
                                                  (trans. by Richard Howard)
† Hope glimmers like wisps of straw in the shed . . .

For an Herbarium

me. I never saw Erik Satie, who dismissed one of my husbands with a wave of his hand. Never saw Maupassant, who felt honor-bound to plunge into the Marne after one of those dinners known as "Scrubbers' Bamboulas" and not die of congestion as a result. Never met the arrogant scaly remnants of Barbey d'Aurevilly . . . Yet for several years I had the leisure of being their contemporary, if not their friend, of being simply one who had seen them. I value no document as I do the memory of the human face, the lingering impression of its color, the incision of the pupil, the radiant wheel of the iris, the forehead covered or bare, the mouth and its successive deteriorations, a mouth unfit to recite its own poem; but it was from just such a mouth that I would like to have heard:

Lys! et l'un de vous tous . . .

This lily to which today I owe my modest divagation stands on the mantelpiece, its one foot in water. With a pair of embroidery scissors, the florist has removed its little hammers of yellow pollen, without which it stands there, clean, mutilated, and sad. Prior to it, all winter long, we could have had—for a price—the greenish lily, which blesses the union of so many young English brides and grooms. Perfidiously scented, the greenish lily can also speak and petition, imploring a disinclined virgin to love. I know nothing more about it, rarely associating with any but the white lily, which I call, wrongly, the true lily. This one here is white, fleshy, long-legged, and for floribundance fears none. It is a terrible pity that it is nearly always infested with Crioceris. The Crioceris is the red kiki, and the red kiki is the Crioceris. If you close a kiki up in your hand, it immediately makes a plaintive little cry with its wing sheath. The only time you call it Crioceris is when it fouls the lily with its dejecta, in the garden.

The true lily's favorite soil is the kitchen garden's, with tarragon, sorrel edgings, and purple garlic for neighbors. A patch of carrots, and a few nice rows of lettuce, yes, it likes that, too. In the garden of my childhood, its dazzling blooms and its fragrance were lords of the garden. While I was out hunting the red kiki, Sido, my mother, sitting inside the house, would call out to me, "Shut the garden door a little, those lilies are making the drawing room uninhabitable!"

And she would let me harvest them like hay and carry them in sheaves to Mary's altar when it was time for the May crowning. The church was stuffy and hot, and the children were laden with flowers. The unruly smell of the lilies would grow thick and interfere with the singing of the hymns. Several of the faithful would get up and rush out; some would let their heads droop and then fall asleep, overcome by a strange drowsiness. But the plaster Virgin, standing on the altar, would be brushing, with the tips of her dangling fingers, the long, half-open cayman jaws of a lily at her feet, smiling down at it indulgently.

For an Herbarium

THE GARDENIA'S MONOLOGUE

Six o'clock . . . Or so claims the white nicotiana. But the white nicotiana is prone to error. It will be six o'clock when I decree that it is six o'clock. Only then will the terrace, the garden, the entire universe be smothered in my perfume.

Six o'clock, well, not quite . . . All I am concerned with is my waking, and I am slow to wake. I am a long time in proclaiming the confidence and clearheadedness that assure my reign from nightfall to the darkness of first light, faintly cut into the east like a brown and purple wound.

The day now drawing to a close was a long one. While it lasted, I held my breath, the exhalation of which surrounds me at dusk and makes the moths teeter and fall into flight. I was sleeping, in my fleshy petals, loosely done up, just mussed enough so no one would confuse me with the bland neatness of the camellia. I sleep in broad daylight, as do all things white and possessed of the secret of scent. For those of us with white blooms, charged with the task of troubling human beings, midday is a treachery we never tire of. It is then that innocent girls, ignorant girls, absentminded girls in love break off one of our flowered stems with their nails and fasten it, all cold and with no more expression than a buttercup, in their hair or at their waists. There I sleep scentless. But at the appointed hour—"six o'clock!"—I let out my feverish, mute discourse. An imaginary orange blossom and an edible mushroom, one hour old and fully grown, come together within me, to the perdition, it would seem, of bodies and souls. The innocent turns into a nanny goat, the absentminded lover blushes and runs away—but not alone!—and the ignorant girl throws herself into a science I have taught her, and the round world reckons one more night of folly.

It is six o'clock. The greening whiteness of my petals still tolerates the fact that close by, in what little daylight is left, can be made out the white nicotiana, the drab pittosporum and oleafragrans, the Bouvardia, delicious but a little slow, the oversized and fragile buds of the magnolia—it cannot possibly be her flesh that Swinburne praises as "fairer for a fleck," the gentle rain from the catalpa, the sand lily which drinks sea water for lack of better, and the jasmine, nearly as luminous as a star. I put up with all these humbler bearers of nocturnal balms, certain that I have no rivals, save one, I confess . . . before whom at times I do worse than confess: I abdicate. On certain meridional nights heavy with the promise of rain, certain afternoons rumbling with casual thunder, then my ineffable rival need only show herself, and for all the gardenia in me, I weaken, I bow down before the tuberose.

For which she shows not the least gratitude. The bloom on her, fresh as a budding nipple, outlasts mine. She holds it up to me, insinuating that I age poorly and that three days after I blossom I look like a white kid glove dropped in the gutter.

ORCHID

I see a small pointed sabot, very pointed. It is fashioned out of a green, jadelike material, and on the tip of the shoe's nose is painted, in maroon, the figure of a tiny nocturnal bird, two big eyes and a beak. Inside this sabot, all along the sole, someone—but who?—has sown a silvery grass, slantwise. The tip of the sabot is not empty, for some hand—but whose?—has spilled a drop of something there, mirrory, glasslike, unlike either natural dew or the artificial dew from the florist's atomizer. I've collected it on the sharp point of my all-purpose blade, my trusty servant that shrinks from no task, that sharpens pencils, peels chestnuts, cuts peri-winkle paper into rectangles and black radishes into disks. In order to get to know this translucid, congealed drop-let better, I've put it on my tongue. As I did so, my best

For an Herbarium

friend raised his voice and his arms. "Poor wretch!" he cried out. To which he added a lovely little speech about the poisonous plants of Malaysia and the ever-mysterious preparation of curare. While awaiting the death throes promised me, I began, with the help of a large magnifying glass, to decipher the orchid. It was brought to me by my daughter, who by way of thanks received a scolding.

"Couldn't you have asked the florist the name of this monster?"

"I did, Mama."

"And what did she tell you?"

"She said, 'Well, I wouldn't feel right repeating it to you. Because when it comes to unusual names, this one's got a humdinger.'"

The droplet, now minuscule, has not dissolved on my tongue. All I have noticed is a very faint taste of raw potato.

Around the little shoe diverge five asymmetrical green arms, speckled with maroon. A beautiful labellum, white at the base, shaped somewhat like the tongue of an iris, opens out beneath them, with a violet stippling applied to it, in the shape, yes, the shape of the pouch-like body of an octopus, for, in fact, my orchid *is* an octopus: if not the eight arms, it does have the parrot beak of the octopods, the beak which a moment ago I called the tip of the sabot.

Only five arms. Who amputated the other three? Who? Where? Beneath what skies? With what in mind? With what license is his mimicry practiced?

Calm down, calm down. Why all the excitement

over a flower from the antipodes, the extravagant cousin of our own vernal hornet orchis, and our ophrys, which looks so amusingly like a corset, with the tiny waist and wings of a wasp! The more inaccessible the wonders of the world around us become, the more extreme its curiosities. I don't mean to complain, not at all. Today's orchid is a distorted dream to me, and most attractive. It speaks to me of an octopus, a wooden shoe, a silvery beard, an owl, dried blood . . . It would have seduced and carried off many far wiser than myself, to mention only a big-game hunter from the last century, one of those small, silent types who bureaucratically kill the flowery-robed jaguar in impossible countries. He shot only jaguars—and now and then a few plump doves to stay alive.

One day, posted by his native beaters on a jaguar path, he grew tired of waiting. Raising his head, he saw above him an orchid . . . a particular orchid. One that definitely resembled a bird, a crab, a butterfly, an evil spell, a sexual organ, and perhaps even a flower. Bedazzled, the great cat hunter set down his rifle and began to climb, not without risk to his life. He conquered the orchid and climbed back down just in time to see coming toward him, toward his weaponless hands, a lordly jaguar, hale and hearty, moist with dew, which dreamily sized the man up and continued on its way.

I am told that this same hunter, who hunted around 1860, later turned into a botanist. What I would like to know is whether he was converted out of gratitude toward the merciful jaguar, or whether the orchid, whose spell is more powerful than that of any other game, had

For an Herbarium

plunged him forever into those regions where a man, caught between two dangers, never fails to choose the greater.

THE WAYS OF
THE WISTARIA

I hope that it is still alive, and that it will go on living for a long time, that flourishing, irrepressible despot, a centenarian at least twice over: the wistaria that spills over the garden walls of the house where I was born, and down into the rue des Vignes. Proof of its vitality was brought to me last year by a spry and charming lady pillager . . . A black dress, a head of white hair, a sexagenarian agility—all this had jumped, in the rue des Vignes, deserted as in bygone days, until it had grabbed hold of and made off with one of the wistaria's long terminal withes, which ended up flowering in Paris, on the divan bed where I am bound by my arthritis. Besides its fragrance, the butterfly-shaped flower retained a small hymenoptera, an inchworm, and a ladybug, all direct and unexpected from Saint-Sauveur, in Puisaye.

For an Herbarium

To tell the truth about this wistaria, in which I discovered, here on my bed table, a fragrance, a blue-violet color, and a bearing all vaguely recognizable, I remember that it had a bad reputation all along that narrow domain bounded by a wall and defended by an iron railing. It dates from long ago, from before my mother Sido's first marriage. Its mad profusion in May and its meager resurgence in August and September perfume my earliest childhood memories. It was as heavy with bees as with blossoms and would hum like a cymbal whose sound spreads without ever fading away, more beautiful each year, until the time when Sido, leaning over its flowery burden out of curiosity, let out the little "Ah-hah!" of great discoveries long anticipated: the wistaria had begun to pull up the iron railing.

As there could be no question, in Sido's domain, of killing a wistaria, it exercised, and exercises still, its decided strength. I saw it lift an impressive length of railing up out of the stone and mortar, brandish it in the air, bend the bars in plantlike imitation of its own twists and turns, and show a marked preference for an ophidian intertwining of bar and trunk, eventually embedding the one in the other. In time it met up with its neighbor the honeysuckle, the sweet, charming, red-flowered honeysuckle. At first it seemed not to notice, and then slowly smothered it as a snake suffocates a bird.

As I watched, I learned that its overwhelming beauty served a murderous strength. I learned how it covers, strangles, adorns, ruins, and shores up. The Ampelopsis is a mere boy compared with the coils, woody even when new, of the wistaria . . .

I visited the Désert de Retz one beautiful, torrid day when everything conspired toward a siesta and disturbing dreams. I will never go back there, for fear of finding that that place, made for tempered nightmares, has paled. Muddy, rush-filled water slept there at the foot of a kiosk furnished with broken-down writing tables, footless stools, and other unexplained pieces of furniture floating around. I cling to the memory of a truncated tower, topped off abruptly by a beveled roof. Inside, it was divided into little cells around a spiral staircase, each of which assumed, roughly, the shape of a trapezoid . . .

O world, how full you are of mysteries and inconveniences for one by no means a born geometrician, struggling in vain to describe the truncated tower of the Désert de Retz! It was crammed with ruined furniture. Should I laugh at their skeletons or fear that one of life's baleful remnants . . .

The sudden shattering of a windowpane made me shudder, and decided it: a vegetable arm, crooked, twisted, in which I had no difficulty recognizing the workings, the surreptitious approach, the reptilian mind of the wistaria, had just struck, broken, and entered.

For an Herbarium

TULIP

Moi, je suis la Tulipe, une fleur de Hollande.

Mais la nature, hélas, n'a pas versé d'odeur
*Dans mon calice fait comme un vase de Chine.**

The other eleven lines of the sonnet are gone from my memory. It is not a great loss, even though its real author is none other than Théophile Gautier. You will find "La Tulipe" in *Un Grand Homme de province à Paris*, in which Balzac attributes it to his hero, Lucien de Rubempré, that ever-so-handsome young man, who wanted to be a poet and famous to boot. He hoped to achieve glory with a collection of sonnets, but only one

* I am the Tulip, a flower from Holland.

But, alas, no scent has nature to place
In my calix shaped like a Chinese vase.

man has been crowned with success in that venture—
José María de Heredia.

Balzac, who wrote only in prose, searched high and
low for sonnets; he was never refused them, but his
poet friends did not give him the pick of their gardens.
For his part, Théophile Gautier painted him a "Tulip."

The firm, smooth touch, the endearing portliness,
and the casual lyricism of the good Théo are all present
in the least of his compositions, even in this one.

It is with him that I wish to pick a horticulturist's, if
not a finicky botanist's, quarrel here, and to ask him if he
has ever seen a Chinese vase shaped to resemble a tulip.
An egg, granted. A tattered flame, fine, if the tulip is of
the so-called parrot species. A rose window, if, in the
heat and extremity of flowering, the beautiful petals are
forced open, near exhaustion, like a wheel; but a Chinese
vase—never! An unyielding hip inflicts the curve of a
waistline on the vases of celestial ceramists. At the home
of José María Sert I saw vases, big enough for a lover to
hide in, that came from China. From a short distance,
their silhouette was that of a large naked woman who,
though headless, stood upright nonetheless, but as for
evoking the calix of a tulip . . .

But come, tulip I deride, come and sit here by my
side. Come painted like an Easter egg, red and streaked
with yellow and orange. Your heavy bottom sits firm on
your stem, and in your center you hide the black-and-
blue bruise that marks the scarlet poppy in the same place.

When tulips are arranged in flower beds by the thousands, the likes of you are remarkably alike, equal in size
and height, straight on your scapes, each with one, and

For an Herbarium

only one, bloom. In your battalions you are the one bright spot in the flat, hardworking, wet Netherlands. Your protocol allows you only two long leaf-ears, bluish-green and always a little downcast . . . I confess that I warm to your intense colors with a kind of respect.

At one time fashion and wild speculation wanted you black, and you fetched a high price. The deeper your blue-violet mourning was, the more your lovers ruined themselves for you. Then came a time of famine, and people cooked your precious bulbs for food. More recently, you served a nobler purpose: during the bad springs under the Occupation, Paris, bursting with hope and embittered with deep resentment, was selling bulbs in its flower shops—three to a pot—which found a way to be seditious. "A pretty pot of tulips, madame, to grow in your apartment?" March came and the oniony nacre awoke, splitting its dry envelope, from which, in place of tulips, there issued forth three gallantly chauvinistic hyacinths—one blue, one white, one red.

"FAUST"

When it was still a novelty, its name won it as much success as its strangeness. The black pansy "Faust" dates from about a half century ago. Gounod's score had, by that time, made its way into the provinces. It was our family's old Aucher piano, and the fingers of my two older brothers, that taught *Faust* to what few instruments there were in our hillside village. "*Salut, ô mon dernier matin! . . . Ne permettrez-vous pas, ma belle demoiselle . . . Et je vois passer les bateaux . . .*" and, at last, the entirety of what one radio program, in 1948, seems frequently quite proud to recall to mind. "*Anges purs, anges radieux . . .*" (One is always a bit nervous for the soprano, isn't one, when she comes to the ascensional moment of the "Rosalie" passage?)

"Faust," the black pansy, has come to pay me its

For an Herbarium

Easter visit. Here it is, on my table, only slightly less black than my black velvet jacket. When the sun strikes it, it is imbued with a dusting of constellations, revealing the fact that the reigning principle behind so much blackness is a blue, no, purple, no, blue so substantial that it wins our admiration. "It's like velvet! . . ." And then? And then nothing. And then we begin again: "It's like velvet!" For we have no word other than velvet with which to depict velvet, whether or not the subject is the "Faust" pansy, with its five petals, all one color, dark as the butterfly wings that spread above the banks of the Amazon.

(How I love to parade my entomological erudition, I who shall never set eyes on either the Amazon or its banks. Especially when I've forgotten the butterfly's name!)

"Faust" first appeared, in pansy form, in a round clump in my childhood garden, near the pump, the weeping ash, and the cherry tree from Montmorency. My parents' friends would come to see it for its blackness and exclaim, "Will you save a few seeds for me? Oh, it's like velvet! . . ." A little eye, intensely yellow, at the center of each flower, would look out at us.

Visitors gone, Sido, my mother, would turn away from the "Fausts." Fickle after her own fashion, she made no secret of the fact that a clump of flowers is not a funeral arrangement, that the red pyrethrums, the azure aconites, the all-wool ageratum, a very dark clematis that used to climb to the top of the walnut tree for the sheer pleasure of letting itself tumble down when it grew dizzy, are all infinitely more lovable. That instead of seeking out funereal "Fausts," a clump of pansies ought to abide by tradition and perpetuate the classical varieties, such as those big, silly, half-yellow, half-purple beauties, those white faces with the garnet-colored mustaches, the lemon-yellow butterfly pansies, those little cornuta, rivals of the violet and Sido's favorites above all others, as full-bodied as Henry VIII, with bearded chins, all staring up at you at once.

"Look at them," Sido would say to me. "Wide as my hand!"

That is because she had a small hand.

"Rather common, but dignified. Self-satisfied, with a fierce brow. And quick to degenerate . . . In short," she concluded, "all the qualities of royalty!"

For an Herbarium

FŒTIDA

They're here, they've arrived, the peonies you say smell like roses, heralds of the first roses. Give plenty of water to these luxurious corollas, which do, indeed, have something of the rose about them—something, but not its fragrance.

Garnet red, bright pink, sentimental pink, and three or four other carmine reds, they are the colors of good health and will delight me throughout the coming week. And then, all at once, they will drop their brazier of petals with a floral sigh imitating the sudden demise of the rose. Its demise, but not its fragrance. For the peony does not smell like a rose, but I will be the last to reproach it for that. The peony smells like a peony. Can't you take my word for it, rather than forever searching for comparisons—attributing to fresh butter the taste of hazelnuts, to pineapple the taste of wild strawberries, and to wild strawberries the sweet, appetizing flavor of crushed ants?

Peonies smell like peonies, which is to say, like cock-chafers. With the aid of a slightly fetid odor, the peony has the privilege of putting us in touch with the true spring, bearer of many suspect odors, the sum of which is likely to leave us enchanted. The lilac, before it blooms, when it is still merely little leaves shaped like the ace of spades and tiny promises of thyrsi, the lilac has the distinct smell of scarab beetles, until the moment of blossoming, frothing, white, mauve, blue, purple, when it fills the suburban trains, the Métro, and children's strollers with its toxic aroma of prussic acid. Then I long for the fragrance of the lilac before it blooms, the smell of its tender, still brown leaves, the fugacious breath, both slightly agreeable and repugnant, of the metallic elytron. So, in the name of spring, which I malign so gravely, you will cease to like me and refuse to understand me. So, I retire deep into my modest antrum, along paths embroidered with, for example, the wild geranium known as herb Robert, its florets insignificant, its seeds shaped like a crane's bill. If you should accidentally graze it with your fingertips, it will leave a spicy scent, too sharp for your liking. I myself crush its purplish leaves and stems on purpose, which sets me dreaming—as one of my cats used to dream over the mysterious messages from freshly tanned leather: she would nose around some and then move on. She would come back and shilly-shally about, swishing her tail, and the perform-ance would end in a series of small retchings, modestly

For an Herbarium

repressed. I do not go quite that far with my herb Robert. I could name other plants most of you would find repellent, whereas I split them with my nail and sniff the white blood of the spurge, the ocher-tinged juice of the celandine called bloodroot.

I prefer the harsh scent that rises from a slightly sinister, slightly medicinal, hence, slightly poisonous herb to the insipid elder, even to the privet, so charged with sweetness that in full flower it keeps us at a respectful distance along the paths at Cancale. And what about the bark of the wild black cherry, do you scorn it? I actually find its aroma pleasing. But how many bottled perfumes have disappointed me! To make up for it, there is the wild onrush that in summer rises from chlorophylls set free in a storm, the iodine released at every low tide, the belch let out by the vegetable garden when it can't hold it back any longer, or by the refuse heap, where black-currant marc, uprooted fennel, and old dahlia bulbs all ferment together—what incense for my independent and capricious sense of smell . . .

Now what was I going to tell you? That the peony has a fragrance, not of peonies or roses, but of cock-chafers? That the lilac, if too near the bedroom, makes a coarse, hydrocyanic lover? That tansy, "the malodorous tansy," as the botanists say, and yarrow put heart back in my stomach, and in my heart, too, and that on the contrary, heliotrope, with its nauseating vanilla and its mauve semi-mourning, disagrees with me? My goodness, that didn't take many lines and words, now that I've said it.

"SOUCI"

"Souci, Souci . . ."

At the call, she would come, proudly bearing the name we give both a flower and our woes. She would come running, with her little bulldog forehead folded and wrinkled, and her ears pricked up like the cornets of the arum. She had a sort of passion for obedience, which still allowed her all her strong personality, her freedom of opinion and choice. She always tried to understand what I was saying before I came to the end of my sentence. She would state firmly, having barely glimpsed him, that such-and-such a person wasn't worth the rope to hang him with, or else that something might be made of him yet. Jealous of Last Cat, she hoped to hide her jealousy by shutting, over her strongly protruding eyes, which slanted up at the temples, over the eyes of a First-

For an Herbarium

Prize-under-Seven-Kilos-Class French bulldog, by shutting, as I was saying, her eyelids just enough to cover two globes spangled like gold aventurine. But she knew perfectly well I was not to be taken in, and thought that perhaps, in some other life, I had once been a bulldog myself, that she would do well to be on her guard with me, to throw me off the scent: who is one to deceive if not those one loves? "Souci, Souci . . ." The well-named one, brow furrowed, pulse irregular, breath shallow, sleep troubled with dreams. Souci, whose left foreleg would tremble beneath the weight of some terrible thought, when a shooting pain, always the same, the sin of loving just one person, would set her blood surging and shake the oversensitive nerves of a bulldog bitch who could suffer for, and because of, me and me alone. To suffer from absence, to suffer from waiting, to suffer from love, is all one. She had determined to repress all signs of physical suffering with casual aloofness. What's a crushed paw? Nothing. A cut, a cactus spine? Even less. And the scraping of the tartar off her teeth, barely worth a throaty growl when the scraper touched a loose molar . . . So thought Souci, the well-named, who is no more.

In February, every February, one of my friends who learned to appreciate Souci sends me a tight bunch of yellow *soucis*, leaving out those that affect the orange-red of the pumpkin. Every year I keep them happy for a few hours in a gray vase with a good coarse glaze on it, ever so slightly bubbled, a big pot where the butter was kept when there was butter. Souci has no grave except in my memory; no tombstone, no epitaph commemorates her virtues, or the dates of her too short life. But these *soucis*, these marigolds and I, we remember her, discreetly. Yellow and perfectly round, the flowers' shape in no way resembles Souci the bitch. Six, seven concentric rows of close petals shaped like plumules cluster tightly around a stamened center, the outer edge of each plumule delicately scalloped. These are flowers and not symbols of a long and perfect canine friendship.

Yet I cannot help but notice that the center, the heart, the eye of this marigold is a lustrous bronze-brown, just as were a pair of beautiful eyes, the color of aventurine . . .

For an Herbarium

BLUE

Apart from monkshood aconite, one squill, one lupine, the *Nigella* called love-in-a-mist, germander speedwell, lobelia, and convolvulus, which triumphs over all blues, the Creator of all things proved himself rather tight-fisted when he was handing out blue flowers here below. Understand that I am not trying to shortchange blue, I simply do not wish to be taken in by it. The grape hyacinth is no more blue than the Monsieur plum . . . The forget-me-not? As it flowers, it doesn't care if it tends toward pink. The iris? Bah! . . . Its blue barely rises above a very pretty mauve, and I won't even speak about the one called "Flame," whose liturgical purple and profane perfume invade the mountain pastures around La Garde-Freinet in spring. The garden iris, at home in all soils, bathes its feet in the little canals of Bagatelle and mixes well with its cousin, the fiery and ephemeral tiger flower. It has six petals, three narrow, smooth tongues, and three wider ones with a thin yellow coating—its liver, no doubt—and it passes for blue, thanks to the unanimity of a host of people who know nothing about the color blue.

There are connoisseurs of blue just as there are lovers of wine. Fifteen consecutive summers in Saint Tropez were not only a "Cure d'Azur" but a course of study as well, which was not restricted to the contemplation of the Provençal sky and did not limit itself to the Mediterranean either. I would not go and beg for blue from the bright beds of fine sand where the waves find rest, knowing perfectly well that, just born of daybreak, the blue of the sea would be cruelly eaten away by an insidious green that extinguishes the last star from the sky, and that each cardinal point, forsaking this fleeting blue, chooses its own celestial color: the east is violet, the north a frozen pink, the west a glowing red, and gray the south. At the height of a Provençal day, the zenith wears an ashen crown. Short shadows huddle under the trees and crouch at the foot of the wall, birds silent, the cat lapping one by one the drops from the fountain spout; at the noon hour every particle of our vital ration of blue and of serenity is in jeopardy.

We would wait for a little wing of dust to flutter at the bends in the road; a white curliness at the lip of the gulf was the sign for all blues to be resurrected. One, the color of hard lapis, now back in the sea, would come bounding, reflected under the arbor, and each glass

For an Herbarium

goblet suddenly would be cradling a cube of sapphire-tinted ice.

On the tops of the still-gilded Alps, a stormy, cottony mass, blue as a ring dove, would be touching the peaks. In a few hours the full moon would make its way through a snow of stars, and until dawn the white sand lilies, closed by day, would be blue.

LACKEE AND POTHOS

You would be mistaken to think this the title of a Hindu apologue. It is merely the legend on one of those large colored plates, a bit yellow and crumbled around the edges, the jetsam of a pretty entomological collection dispersed by vandalism and improvidence. In the old days, I bought them whenever I came across them. This one is signed Bessa, that one Geneviève de Nangis, another one Denisse, painter and lithographer. I learn from them only what I want to learn. What minute detail! I can count the hairs on the wide tongues of the irises, the pustules on the grainy, digitate lemons, and to facilitate study, science will dismember the floral organs of the carnation, the crocus, Good-King-Henry or clary, common speedwell, and brooklime.

I wander through the numbered petals, the dis-

For an Herbarium

jointed stamens, the pleasantly sexual germ cells, and the manelike roots. I learn nothing, I just gaze. All the texts have perished. No other information but the finely engraved address of the artist, and occasionally the publisher; one lived nearby on the *"rue Croix-des-petits-Champs vis-à-vis l'Hôtel de Lussan."* Ah, neighbor! Without this gap of two mean little centuries between us, what delight I would have taken in your work! Thanks to you, a Chinese quince, with its grainy fruit, blistered zinc-blue leaves, and pink flower, all looking as if the watercolors were still wet, is preserved with a hundred-year-old freshness on stiff laid paper, in defiance of time. This pictorial art makes one's mouth water, and the care with which it was rendered has not failed to include, at the bottom of the page, the likeness of three eye-shaped brown pips.

But I have a special grudge against Pothos and Lackee. They come after the "Guava Apple, which grows without any form of cultivation, the apple being used for jelly," and the "Giant Strawberry." Talk about giants, indeed! This particular kind of enormous, reddish organ, "life-size," covers the entire folio. On it one can see the hairy pores, and two breastlike lobes, like those of the sacred hearts of Jesus that bleed in devotional images. Its legend seems not in the least surprised. "The strawberry, called custard apple, is pleasant to eat straight from the tree. Its leaves, when boiled, will cure stomach ailments."

I had hoped for more from this giant and its properties when I acquired its image a good thirty-five years ago. On the following page, Pothos and Lackee, conjugate, assuage my thirst for the improbable. The one drips with pyriform fruit, crimson among camellia foliage, and its flowers—Lackee's, that is—tinged with pink, marbled with blue, in such a way that I suspect the painter, the explorer, and the botanist of having done their traveling in their dreams . . . Then my faith is restored and I believe, unshakably, that the Lackee "rises to a height of forty-five feet in a very short time. It produces fruit best eaten fricasseed, which has the taste of veal or chicken."

Bravo! Bravo! Let us drink freely of this marvelous tonic! More, more! Long live the veal of the wilds, the traveler's providence! Why stop there, plant gatherer? Why have you not assured us that, not content to grow in just a few hours, the Lackee is oviparous, that it imitates the voice of the pangolin, attracts and sustains a multitude of fireflies, and serves as a beacon for the lost!

About Pothos the lovely, tattered album says nothing. Looking at the brilliant picture it gives me, I can see that the Pothos is a mighty cucumber, whose emerald epidermis is divided into regular hexagons, like bathroom-floor tile. Each hexagon sports in its exact center another geometric figure in relief, a multicolored jewel; granted, it is a cucumber, but a deluxe one got up like a four-leaf clover . . . No, rather than a clover leaf, I see in it the quadrilobate form of a lilac blossom . . . With the difference that, unlike the lilac flower, and as if to flout elementary common sense, the Pothos, known also as the "Embroidered Pothos," resembles a sausage which . . .

I give up! To attempt to depict, in black and white, the enchantments for which the colors of the spectrum barely suffice, is a fool's game. Disentangle yourself from Pothos and Lackee. Do what their renowned designer-painter did: invent.

LILY OF THE VALLEY

More than a flirtation, better than a superstition, almost a religion, the lily of the valley is celebrated on the first of May. Its cult stirs the Parisian populace to fever pitch, but dies down beyond its suburbs. Further out, the provinces breathe with equanimity the slightly acid scent of the little flower that is totally ignored in the Midi: The caretaker's wife down on my little piece of Provence in Saint Tropez would inquire, "Lily of the valley? What's that?"

But on the first of May, come see the streets of Paris, the assault on the florists, twenty francs a "sprig," a thousand francs a bunch; see them in the men's lapels, at the women's waists, countless witnesses of a belief in "good luck!" But pay a visit to the flower market near the President's Palace in Rambouillet. On the trestle

For an Herbarium

tables the lilies of the valley foam up and spill over in tight bunches. Their long, green leaves ring them like crowns, following a custom no one would dream of questioning.

"What about putting the leaves in the center and the flowers around the outside for a change," I proposed to one woman.

She looked at me as if I had taken leave of my senses, then shrugged her shoulders. "Well, thanks a lot! I'd never sell a single one!" she said.

I once saw some pretty young maids, baskets over their arms, slipping quickly and cautiously into the park at Rambouillet.

"We're going to Albert Lebrun's to steal some of his lilies of the valley," one of them shouted to me.

"And what if you get caught? There are guards!"

"Don't worry! We get along with the guards. They can't stand the sight of the lilies, the seeds kill the pheasant chicks!"

An old huntress of everything the forest produces—bluebells, wild strawberries, hazelnuts, foxgloves, blackberries—would set off "to the lilies" before dawn, pass by the Dutch Ponds and their overtrodden environs, taking care that no one followed her. She would head homeward at the hour when the green forest turns blue. Her long stride, the stride of a robust, aging woman, would set swinging all around her the bunches of lily of the valley hanging head down, twenty, thirty, fifty bunches, each on the end of a lasso of string, like poacher's game. She lightened her load by selling them along the way, and I never failed to supply myself from the stock of this dryad with white hair and white flowers, perfumed and majestic, looking like Louis XIV, and a rustic one at that.

I did not care so much for weekends, with the forest besieged by Paris, the motor trucks whose cargo outbound—fresh bread, pork pâtés, cheese, dixies of red wine, and coffee—was, on the return journey, nothing but pure lilies of the valley, cinched, picked too soon, and greenish like cauliflower. I feared for the broody hen-pheasants, terrified in their nests of dry bracken, and heroic, letting themselves be taken rather than abandon their barely feathered offspring . . . O sweet little hen-pheasant, motionless and warm when my fingers once accidentally came across you . . . I withdrew my hand and whistled very softly to my bitch, who, a few paces away, had picked up the scent of the feathers, and to throw her off, I promised her a lizard, a shrew mouse, a mole, all game whose names she knew—I had not taught her that of the pheasant . . .

We would return at sunset by way of Saint-Léger, through Les Mesnuls, Montfort-l'Amaury, and Neauphle. All the way to Versailles children blazed the trail, brandishing by the fistful bunches of lily of the valley, bluebells, wood anemones, Solomon's seal, blue sage, ground ivy, and veronica (whose eyes lose their azure as soon as they are picked), yellow wallflowers snatched from their old stone niche, and star-of-Bethlehem (called Eleven O'Clock Lady), which closes up if a cloud passes in front of the sun . . .

But we made no more stops, and besides ourselves, the car carried the fragrance of wilted and exhausted

For an Herbarium

flowers, and the combined weight of a little too much enjoyment and a fatigue which, in May, is the reward of a day devoted to the still tender forest and the flowering of the lily of the valley.

RED CAMELLIA

Everything that bears the imprint of immoderation remains with us. Perhaps excess alone suits us, at least during the time appointed for feeling ourselves duly astonished, tempted, desirous, and young. That youth may be the ineluctable agent of temptation does not concern me in the least, not only because I have left it behind, but above all because my youth had other and better things to do than run wild, which is to say that it had to work hard and learn, and keep a tight rein on itself. It set its sights on many different objects, but I did not know the rules of the game to obtain them. Together on the same plane of longing I placed a garden I would one day own in Paris, and a ground-floor apartment, dark and well protected, in whose shadows a wood fire would wave its multicolored peonies. But when I made the ac-

For an Herbarium

quaintance of thirteen performing greyhounds, I did not give the comfortable prison or the garden of a wealthy Parisian another thought. And when I gave up this chimera, this arabesque, this trained hurricane—thirteen white greyhounds—I made do with a Brabançon bitch that, full-grown, weighed one kilo. And so on. As with love. With the same myopic and baroque taste that governs the feeling of love, at once demanding and satisfied with little. With the same languor that comes over me and saddens me in museums where man has assembled too many works of human beauty, with the same exclamatory joy with which I greet the triumph of the purple seed forcing its cotyledons, since it appears to me that it is the seed—and not the museum—that is the real wonder.

And here, once again, is the real wonder, beside me in my room. Six red camellias . . .

Subjected to exceptional cruelty, they will stand up to it for several hours. They will live on air. Their blooms and leaves cling to one another by a mere thread. A brass wire pierces the cupule of the sepals, pierces the vigorous heart abounding in stamens, passes right through it, twists and knots itself around the stem, holding stiff the magnificent, secretly decapitated flower, which will end its life standing up.

Six red camellias. On the bad days of each month, *La Dame aux Camélias* would arrange them in her beautiful consumptive's hair—which she kept long, black, and silky—as a sign to the crowd that she was sleeping alone. A certain deplorable taste, a certain shamelessness know no limits and, strangely enough, are tolerated. Six red camellias . . . In my primary school, for classroom decorations on Awards Day, Mademoiselle Olympe Terrain taught us how to make camellias out of red paper, we who had never in our young lives set eyes on a camellia, not even in a painting. So that our flowers, of a rather arbitrary opulence, suffered distortions that actually may have been embellishments.

What six red camellias can do for me now is take me back to those that have outlived them, back to their chosen ground. In the climate of Brittany, over the last hundred years, an arbor has slowly been formed, like a varnished cemetery. Black in shadow, blacker still in the sun, each leaf letting in only one spot of pale-blue light on its convex surface, they await the moment, the still cold season when, all at once, the camellias blaze red.

The hour of decay follows hard on their red climax. Prevented from ever seeing them again where they bloom, I tell myself that at least there no rusty wire forces the weight of a heavy flower on its weakening stem. There it is the slightest Breton breeze, the hoof of a dun cow, the shower brought by the incoming tide, that strew the ground with a rain of red camellias . . .

For an Herbarium

HYACINTHS

I have been assured that over toward Marly, in the forest,
beneath the dead leaves, the horns of the bluebells are
already as long as my finger. Warning signs, as much as
promises, on the fifth of January 1948. I gather the fore-
casts from the mouths of the informed who set off on
weekends "to see how spring is coming along." Now,
in fact, it *is* coming along, to a varied reception. One
silly woman claps her hands. "The elders are turning
green! We'll be camping by Easter!" But a wiser one
lowers her eyes: "And the buds of the chestnuts already
changing shape. And daisies in the meadows already. And
the buds of the lilacs swelling. We'll be in a fine fix, come
the April moon."

I listen, I take in this and that. Before, I mean before

I was hobbled by this leg of mine, I was the one who would send up the cry, whether of alarm or joy. On the banks of the choppy water at Les Vaux-de-Cernay, I was the one who bundled up the leaves that fell in November and who examined the pale little rostra poked up by the anxious bulbs. Today, my gloomy privilege has fetched me, before anyone else, a bouquet of white hyacinths. It is they, in their green vase, who scent my room. They have already drunk so much in the glass house they were born in, and have so distended their avid veins that the least shock injures them. Their thick spikes, swollen with water, ooze where cut, like a snail, and bear little bells, heavy and opaque, as white as peppermint candy. What do they have in common with the tall, spindly daughter of the woods, ravaged though never destroyed each spring by the Parisian populace, what do they have in common with the wild hyacinth, the blue-bell? Picked ruthlessly, immoderately, it hangs its head, loses its faint scent, and dies. It must be seen only while it lives, and in multitudes, through the still bare copse, and of a blue spread so evenly that from a distance you are deceived: "Look, a pond . . ."

But, O my fat, white, cultivated hyacinth, born in a sitz bath shaped like a carafe that cradled your bulb while it slept there on the table among the cat, the teapot, and the schoolboy's exercise books—O my well-padded little city dweller, my thanks to you for standing in for what I do not and henceforth will not ever have—that blue forest flourish, spontaneous and fragile, in numbers

For an Herbarium

great enough for me to draw from it the illusion that I was standing on the edge of a lake or a field of blue flax in flower . . .

ANEMONE

Heaven knows, Redouté painted it! He put into it all the skill, detail, and exactitude he knew and taught to the Dauphine Marie Antoinette. Having finished the flower, he added the drop, the cabochon of dew, which he placed on it like a bewitching beauty mark. It was from him that princesses learned to paint and anemones to weep. The anemone, and the hundred roses, and the bear's-ear, everything in nature with a velvet bloom melts into tears under Redouté's brush, and I am reminded of the emotion with which Madame Vigée-Lebrun, when it came time to write her *Memoirs*, dipped her pen in the bitter water of her beautiful eyes . . .

The anemones here with me now are dry-eyed. In December they left the Nice Horticultural, that stern

For an Herbarium

industry which means business with flowers and does not see the poetry in a disarray of corollas and a riot of colors. They made the trip without a drink and did not die, but simply fainted. They reached me prostrate, closed, and at first showed only the undersides of their petals, colorless, fluted, slightly haired, and their thick parsley leaves, which hark back to the kitchen garden rather than to the flower bed. And what of the pale promises of scarlet, pink, and purple made to me even as they swooned? Would they, my Provençales snatched from the winter sun, ever keep them?

A warm footbath, and almost by leaps and bounds they revive. Majesty of the round flower! The asymmetrical iris hesitates, then splits its silk cover with an uneven tongue. At times the rose suffocates in its corselet, but the anemone's gesture is magnificently decisive. When the veins of its stem are irrigated, it opens all at once, like a parachute seized by a gust of wind. I would also compare it to the twilight moth named *Likenée*, which, throwing off the day's slumber behind a Venetian blind or on the trunk of a pine tree, stretches out its first pair of gray wings and then suddenly unfurls its skirt, raspberry red hemmed with black or moonlight blue with a dark trim, for the night's revels.

Each anemone, feeling more like itself, is at present a surprise of red velvet, of uncompromising purple; two or three "rarities" are streaked, like a tulip, a near-maroon and not-quite-garnet. A lovely fire on a shut-in's table! I love flowers, certainly. But I love animals no less; no

doubt the anemones know this, for they have brought
me, in each full-blown center, a pretty little hedgehog
of stamens, blue.

For an Herbarium

BROWSINGS

The promoter of La Poubelle Délicieuse had crowned himself with an Aryan name—Louis Forest. In actual fact, he was the most likable Israelite you could ever set eyes on, clever, patient, a good storyteller, a gourmet, and a gourmand. Only the overstrict application of a principle tripped up his eloquent gastronomy in several essays about which I can say only that they were culinary and did not long excite the public's curiosity.

To eat, cooked, the tops of carrots; to nibble, raw, the leaves of the radish along with the radish; to salvage the leafage of viper's grass, young nettles, and the rootstock of rushes; to find a place in the salad for the roots of the lesser celandine and the sprouts of the marsh samphire—and I could mention many others even more bitter—such was the mission to which, during the last war, Louis Forest brought his ingenuity, if not his entire good faith, to bear.

I can recall several banquets at La Poubelle Délicieuse. Those agapes ended better than they began, for after the dessert of dried fruits, cakes made without eggs or flour, and a mushy compote of barberries, Louis Forest would pour us coffee, prepared in a *"caféolette"* of his own invention, that never met with a single detractor.

Besides greens and spicy-tasting wild herbs, our friend preached the alimentary virtues of certain corollas, guaranteeing them, after a few fair tries, unanimous approval. But no militant or aspiring "Poubelliste" ever consented to ingest the rose-petal salad, which dragged the decorative nasturtium down with it into disrepute. I myself had already withdrawn my regard for the latter, for its peppery and slightly blistering savor, and I will allow only the climbing, creeping, graceful nasturtium, with its pointed little crest, scarlet beneath its round, bluish leaf that welcomes, without ever getting wet, the drip of the watering can and the pearls of rain. I liked it thick in my country gardens, and in Provence I married it to the pale-blue plumbago, the two of them entwining their tresses and their colors, one with the other, in love.

For those greens that we deny the status of food, we make room on the hors d'oeuvre dish, in the pickle jar, and in the earthenware keg where the mysterious *mère* of the vinegar slumbers and swells. Late in the season, when the nasturtium sheds its flowers and puffs up its seeds, I would pack it off to join the button capers filched from Segonzac's caper bush, the plump stalks of sea fennel, the aborted little melons, the puny carrots, a few stringy green beans, the verjuice grapes—a whole season's surplus stock which, giving up the idea of growing rich in sugar, would release its pale properties into the vinegar, in hopes of later brightening up the melancholy of cold veal and breaking down the last resistance of a big salt beef.

THE ADONIAD AT THE CONCIERGE'S LODGE

A heartrending cry, in the distance: "Adonis is dead! Adonis is dead! Oh, Adonis! . . ."

"Who is that wailing up there like that?"

"It's the lady upstairs, because Adonis is dead."

"Adonis is dead? Ah, such is life! Accidents happen so quickly!"

"Especially hunting accidents . . . But he just had to go and horse around behind the boars . . . Boars'll turn on you . . . And no one's going to convince me there's not a woman out for revenge behind it all."

The voice: "Adonis . . . Oh, Adonis . . ."

"Can you hear her up there? All night long it was nothing but one long cry."

"Oh, she'll get over it. It's not as if this was her first crush or anything."

For an Herbarium

"Such a good-looking young man! And built to live to a hundred!"

"And stark naked like that, right there on the grass, my dear, and no one to dress him or his wounds! And believe it or not, all of a sudden he changed beyond recognition."

"Go on."

"I'm telling you. Metamorphosed they call it. Look, see for yourself: that little blood-red flower in the pot on the windowsill, that's all that's left of him."

"It can't be!"

"It's not that it's ugly, it's just not much to look at. A little flower the size of a pea . . . With a black spot, a black beauty mark, at the base . . ."

"His own, Adonis' own beauty mark, of course!"

"You seem to know more intimate details about the young man than I do, madame."

"Madame, I'm only repeating what I've been told."

"But it might give some people the wrong idea."

"Oh, come on, you're not going to fight over a little flower, are you? A little nothing of a flower, with a lot of green around it to make it look like something!"

The voice: "Adonis! Oh, my world, my all!"

"There's one who disagrees. Just listen to her. She can cry all she wants, it's not going to bring him back. If they had to go and metamorphose him, as you put it, our gods should at least have been able to change him into something a little more substantial, and nicer to look at."

The voice: "Adonis! Adonis is dead!"

"She won't be happy till she's cried us all deaf. How

'bout we change the subject? I have to leave you now, ladies, I'm off to cash my jam coupons."

The voice: "Adonis! Oh, Adonis! Thy blood burgeons on the mossy ground, and this marble, thy breast, which, whiter than Phoebe, lights the clearing dishonored by death . . . Oh, Adonis, forever rooted . . ."

For an Herbarium

JEANNETTE

What a terrific drinker that Jeannette is! "Jeannette" is what she is called where I come from. She is forever thirsty. With the help of her green tube, tender yet crisp, she drinks as through a straw. She sucks up the water from the spongy meadow, she empties the ditch and the "water rings" in the forest, she drains the banks of the temporary stream filled by the winter rains, while early spring can talk of none but her, Jeannette, Jeannette, Jeannette . . .

But sometimes she changes sex and is then called Narcissus. Narcissus puts on a creamy pallor and a crimped ruff, trimmed with red piping, which rests on a bertha of petals . . . Bertha, ruff, piping . . . Am I so short of words that I must take them from those for feminine adornment? No, but the analogy is straight-forward and striking, from petal to frill, from corolla to lace.

As for the *Grande Jeannette*, her hollow trumpet sounds its ivory horn across the meadows, and so we call it "trumpet daffodil." At the base of its *pavillon*, yellow as gold, deep as foxglove's thimble, its family of stamens finds shelter. Its hardy corolla is one big trap of innocent fragrance washed away by the rains, ravaged by the cold, revived by the March sun. A scrap of rumpled silk hangs about its neck—oh, that Jeannette, she never did learn the proper way to tie a cravat! Still, it is only she they want for those big eggs that the flower vendors in Paris sell by the truckload at Easter time. The woman selling them sticks a plume of lance-shaped leaves in the small end of the egg. No one knows why, but tradition demands it. It wouldn't take much more for the daffodil egg to look like a pineapple.

How much I loved, in the Provençal South, the white Jeannettes coming before the yellow ones, and then jonquils with a heavier scent than the orange tree itself! How I loved, there where winter is neither long nor harsh, these harbingers of spring . . . Don't feel sorry for me, I have them here with me today, on my Paris table. They lower the level of the clear water in their vase by drawing it up so greedily that I think I hear them sucking. I have white ones, and I have yellow ones, and Harris has even added a little bunch—oh, surprise!—of pink Jeannettes . . . But I have a sneaking suspicion that

For an Herbarium

before sending them to me, Harris poured into the drinking trough of these intemperate creatures a good glassful of red ink . . .

MEDICINALS

For me it all began with a botanical inclination to learn from being around my brother, the older one, who early on showed promise of a career in medicine, and who loved plants above people, and animals better than any plant. Whenever I set off with him for the countryside, I would let myself believe that I was herborizing. But the only thing I ever tasted was freedom, the marvelous appanage of Sido's children.

In the old days, the medical team of the region I was born in consisted of Dr. Pomié, silver with age and trembling like frost, a small batch of simple bonesetters, tooth pullers, and midwives—about the latter my mother would speak in tones of vituperation and mystery . . . The shapes of the plants and a nomenclature filled with pleasing errors were enough for me back then. Aren't

For an Herbarium

they still? In those days a village never lacked for women who gathered simples. "Just so many death risks!" Sido would say. But I would sneak away and follow them into the woods anyway. They spoke little and smelled good. The aroma of sinful wormwood and mint from the marshes dogged their steps. They were proud old women who valued their prestige. They rarely sat down, and rested on their feet while they knitted, with the tip of the fourth steel needle stuck in the convolutions of a big peach stone hanging at their stomachs on the end of a string, an old stone, handed down from mother to daughter, all shiny from use . . .

Only one embroidered, and that better than words can say. From her eyes, obscured by spectacles, from her hands, boiled in wash water and tisanes, there came forth handkerchiefs with floral initials for fine ladies, baptismal gowns for pampered newborns, veils sculpted into foliage and medallions, and bridal shifts so stiffened by raised satin stitch and Turkish point that they could have stood up on their own, brideless before the groom . . .

Time has destroyed the handiwork of the herborizing embroideress, who was known to everyone only as La Varenne. For many years my mother and I kept several embroidered collars and some handkerchiefs with which there was never any question of wiping our noses. Preserved as if by some miracle, they, too, have now vanished. La Varenne resembled, feature for feature, red and puffy to boot, the fairy godmother, in the Perrault illustrated by Gustave Doré, who hollows out Cinderella's pumpkin-coach.

Such a resemblance added more than a little to the embroideress's charm and authority. If I asked her a question, I had no fear of La Varenne ever hesitating. She would come out with a name—what am I saying?—two, ten names, which she would then comment on.

"This one cures warts . . . This one kills dogs . . . That's snake herb—wherever you see it, you'll see a snake nearby. That furry little leaf, that's rat's-tail cactus."

"Why?"

"Because."

"Because why?"

"Because it's rat's-tail cactus, that's why. That one there is lungwort, for the lungs."

About a little purple cowwheat berry, she instructed me: "You can eat it, it's barberry, you can make jam out of it, too. But you can't plant it near the corn."

"Why not?"

"Government doesn't allow it.* It ruins the corn. This here is greater comfort.† Just like spinach. That little red berry is one of the morellos."

"Is it good?"

"Yes, for vomiting."

"So it's not good?"

"Yes, it's good for vomiting. What's that you've got there? Did you prick yourself? Serves you right. All right, come over here, hold still, let me squeeze the little colt's-fart out of you."

* True, apparently.
† For comfrey, I think.

For an Herbarium

She opened her knife, protected her bare hand with a coarse mitten, and stripped the prickles off one of those impressive thistles with purple candelabra, the wild and woolly brothers of the artichoke. I often ate that tall Onopordon, and I still eat its heart, with a little salt or in a vinaigrette.

When I was little I barely distinguished my desire to learn from the hunger that leads a child to the fuzzy gooseberry, the wild sorrel, and the bloodwort, just as it leads a cat to couch grass. A child knows much less about such things than an animal, especially a carnivore steeped in vegetarian hygiene. My last bulldog bitch, in Saint Tropez, used to pick her remedies seemingly at random, when her need to vomit was so great that she couldn't satisfy it quickly enough. One time she started by eating the prescribed couch grass, salivated, nibbled at a wild apricot sapling, stripping it of all its leaves, then staggered blindly before swallowing a lovely zinnia, leaving its flower untouched, and finally rid herself of her bile, which had been upset by the southern climate. As for the zinnias, I could see that she would make a habit of them.

In one volume of her *Reminiscences*, Marguerite Moreno tells us how the intelligent director of an Argentine zoo used to give blood-cleansing couch grass to his bigger game animals. On the subject of purgatives, La Varenne held nothing back. Diuretics, too, enjoyed a considerable run. What did a few distorted words matter! La Varenne would say santonilla for santonica, and titterwort for tetterwort (Chelidonium). But her errors left the conviction of the faithful unshaken. She could never mention "shepherd's-needle," an unassuming umbellifer, without affecting a strange naughtiness, which grew stranger and naughtier whenever chance found her in the presence of another herbaceous mediocrity, the "shepherd's-sac." I was to learn, much later, that women who no longer have any dealings with love do not easily part with such freedom of allusion.

Without ever confusing species, La Varenne would mutate names. Of those she accommodated to her personal phonetics, several remain with me. Amaurosis, formerly, and dangerously, prepared with the help of the poisonous pasqueflower, became "amorousness," and thus the old narcotic turned aphrodisiac, with all the risks. Caring little that a letter from Boileau to Racine extolled the use of officinal sisymbrium, called "chanter's herb," for loss of voice, our Varenne named it "chancre's herb" and administered it . . . in accordance with her mordant mistake.

Short on science, the clandestine pharmacopoeia does not scruple to improvise. So many "witch's herbs," so many "have-a-boy herbs" . . . Go see for yourself: In the region where I grew up you will still find more "geramions" than geraniums. As its season ends, the violet grows pale: then it is called "dog-eared violet." Mauve-veined on a near-white ground, scentless, small, spindly-legged, no one is interested in it, we are already far removed from the true, the blue violet, which, from February on, blankets the slopes facing south or west. Picked without its stem, it is then laid out on sheets of white paper in the darkness of the attic. They would fill the house I grew up in with a fragrance that, as Sido

For an Herbarium

used to say, "began well and ended badly," before ministering to our autumn colds. If I never knew of a village dwelling that dispensed with the drying of simples, I never once saw my mother make use of them herself. It was from her that I learned to profess that a brew of wild violet had no more taste than faded leaves, that lime blossom . . . Oh my goodness, smell the lime tree when it is a volcano of bees, a mass of russet blossoms, a rival to the orange tree, an insidious lover, a shower of golden pollen, isn't that enough? And when boiled, it is to be responsible for curing your fevers as well? Write its name on the labels of those little square drawers that have round button knobs on their bellies: *violet, lime, verbena, mint, sweet clover, orange petal*, and don't forget *Tussilago*! I am no longer very sure over what ailments the latter extends its tutelary little paw, all fluffy and yellow. But it has such a pretty name! I have also forgotten what, with all due respect, devil's rod is used for, and about a plant that boasted of being the "surgeon's Bible" I remember only the name.

"What's that good for?" I would ask.

La Varenne would scratch her head, under its knotted kerchief, with the tip of her fourth needle, and answer, the fire from her spectacles flashing at the distant woods that harbored fanciful cure-alls and reputedly deadly liquors: "for Nothing."

Today the defunct Varenne has not lost all her powers. Her simples have merely narrowed their sphere of influence. The devil with purges, abortion colics, sleep troublers, and love-vanquishing herbs! But, as you can see, I still call on them for the stuff of dreams.

CALF'S-FOOT ARUM

It is a flower—if you like. But the fact is, I do not like. What makes you think that the arum is a flower? Not a petal, not a sepal in sight. The green of its stem widens out with neither suture nor joint, flares into a cornet, and whitens. The white convolvulus draped over the hedges knows better, the long pendant of the datura is a poisonous jewel. But you like the arum, its minimum of refinement, its stiffness; "What lovely simplicity, what strength," you say . . . Am I trying to pick a quarrel with you or with the arum?

There is also the Strelitzia, whose charms and floral seductions I dispute. Abounding in number and color, they crowded the garden of the Hôtel Saint-Georges in Algiers . . . So much deep blue, and less deep blue, and orange scattered through the crest that fans out at the

For an Herbarium

tip of each stem; so many pointed beaks, which justify the name bird-of-paradise . . . But in the strange, digitate shape of its bloom, I read the exact pose of a Siamese hand, with the tips of thumb and forefinger touching, the other fingers standing straight up, aggressive. In the language of the Siamese ballet, this stiffening of the hand at the end of a dancer's long, supple arm serves, as might a letter of the alphabet, to express anger. Which was the first to imitate the other, the roused hand or the rebellious flower?

Ith, the dancing girl, was beautiful, entitled to all the male roles; beautiful despite all the chalky makeup, the flat, expressionless face, her little nose barely raised above the flesh of her cheeks. As she mimed the part of an angry prince, at every moment her prodigious hands —thumb and forefinger joined, the three free fingers recurved—signified, at the end of her pivoting wrists, the word "wrath," and evoked in me the image of the Strelitzia flower.

I come back, out of lack of sympathy and under-standing, to the other plant that leaves me cold and to which bouquets in the West give pride of place: the arum. In my part of the country, it stands gaping in the damp woods, but there, in its wild state, its cornet remains green, and we call it the monk, because in the center of its rolled trumpet there stands, phallic and brown, a style as big as you please, like a preacher in the pulpit. He does not smell good, this little monk. So leave it in the thick woods around Auteuil where you can still come across it, the spring herald of the big arum made of white kid you are so fond of.

What would you have said, in Tangiers, of the waste ground in front of the new hotel I was staying in, when you saw the usual nettles and the customary couch grass giving way to arums, nothing but arums and more arums? Every day a gang of local ruffians hacked and trampled the big, scentless trumpets. It is always pitiful to see something which asks nothing more than to live being destroyed. I complained to one of the hotel's decorative factotums, who uncrossed his idle arms and shrugged his shoulders.

"It must be," he said. "Is bad weed."

"Poor little arums . . ."

He raised his velvet eyebrows. "Is not laroums," he said. "Is calves' feet."

For an Herbarium

POPPY

So lightheaded! And ringing like a sleigh bell, but far from empty. Beneath its round corona an array of little holes opens up, once it is mature, and sprinkles with a fine black seasoning the well-peppered ground where the next poppy will spring up, next year's poppy, the big scarlet poppy. My goodness, it's all so nice and tidy. Why don't we copy this perfect model of a salt shaker, a pepper mill, or a sugar caster for the strawberries?

The little green parakeets used to peck away at these seeds whenever we left them any, but we rarely did. For the poppy seed, when fully ripe, loses its bitterness and retains an agreeable taste of opiated almonds. As children, we chewed them by the handful, with the promise of a whipping, a stomachache, or a deadly stupor. Did we sleep more because of it? I recall only the ill effects of the hemp seeds, ingested in like manner, after fighting for them with the birds in the bird house. I do remember that the generic savor and smell began at the corn poppies in the fields, grew stronger among the mauve poppies sown in rows and set aside for the pharmacopoeia, and were accompanied by the little music of dry chicken feed beneath the head of the big red poppy, the flaming glory of any flower bed.

This poppy, bruised a deep blue at the base of its scarlet cupule, set proudly in the midst of its native greenery bristling with itchy hairs, is called "Mephisto" by timorous souls. Yet it was in vain that Félix de Vandenesse enlisted it to lead the carnal conquest of Madame de Mortsauf. Rather than dismantle her, the poppy would have put the unhappily married woman to sleep. It is useful in other crimes as well, be it only to pour sleep from bluish bottles into colorless babies.

I left the big poppy, with its blue pollen and its slowly unfolding silk, to the fields and gardens. Long afterward, I came upon it again, in Paris, behind closed doors. Syrupy, black, sequestered, then it was called "the drug" and bubbled cautiously, drop by drop, in an Oriental pipe, among mats, cushions, and recumbent bodies. I recognized its smell, which had never seemed so pleasant, so perfect, a smell that, not content with being so fully itself, makes discreet borrowings from truffles and lightly roasted cacao.

One needn't smoke opium to like opium. Needy addicts can link it up in their minds only with an irreplaceable form of relief. A painful foresight in them measures, counts out and numbers grams and francs, in dread of miscalculation. But to those who love the smell of opium and choose not to smoke fall various pleasures: hour after hour fragrant with tea and tobacco, the occasional touch of a bit of silk or a priceless rug, an unforeseen friendship, and the aegis, which is all it takes to turn the night crimson, of the majestic scarlet poppy.

HELLEBORE

Where we live, and to a lesser extent everywhere else, it is called the Christmas rose. Yet it does not resemble a rose, not even the little eglantine, nervous and blushing, except that it does have five petals like all the others.

A pebble, a blade of grass, a fallen leaf, all have more of a smell than it does. To be fragrant is not its mission. But let December come, let the wintry frost blanket us, and the hellebore will show you its true colors. A nice deep snow, not too powdery, a little heavy, and winter nights that the west wind passes through like a precursor, now that's what makes the hellebore happy. To the garden of my childhood, it was at the end of December that I would go, certain to find it there, and lift the slabs of snow that covered the winter rose.

For an Herbarium

Promised, unexpected, precious, and prostrate but fully alive, the hellebores hibernate. As long as they are weighed down with snow, they remain closed, ovoid, and on the outside of each furled convex petal a vaguely pink streak seems to be the only indication that they are breathing. The hardy, star-shaped leaves, the firmness of the stems, so many characteristics through which the whole plant proclaims its touching, evergreen determination. When picked, its sensitive little shells undo their seams in the warmth of a room, unleashing the little tuft of yellow stamens, happy to be alive and spreading, free . . . Hellebore! When you are put into the hands of the florist, his first concern is to manhandle your petals, bending them back flat, just as he attempts to do to the tulip, torturing it to death. Behind his back, I undo his work of breaking and entering, and if I can promise you, in my house, water up to the neck and light up to the eyelashes, you can sleep out the remainder of your chaste slumber, then perish by the decision of human hands, when the warm snow might still have kept you alive, hellebore.

A NOSEGAY

FROM THE MIDI

I have received a small bundle of almond tree "clippings" from the Midi, sacrificed each year to the rising of the sap. Each branch brandishes its still closed buds; tomorrow, in a vase filled with lukewarm water, their flowers will burst into stars, which seem like dewy wax, and at the same time, they will exhale their winged, honeyed perfume, recognizable among all other perfumes. Happy the Midi! As early as January, it has the jonquil, the almond tree, the mimosa in great yellow clouds, the rustic carnation, and the anemone, while the rest of France is still stiff with cold.

A friend drops by to see me, draws the curtain, makes a sour face at the arbors of bare elms, and sighs, "When will winter ever end?"

I don't bother to inform her that winter no more

has an end than spring has a beginning, and that the earth knows neither death nor rest. Only for the city dweller does winter interject, between October and March, a monolithic season hewn out of a block of wet, gray, leafless months, whitened here and there by thin, patchy snow, signaled by the advent of oysters, concerts, chestnuts, and skis. To those far from the city and steeped in all that varies and does not die, to them alone does each day bring with it the certainty of change, of labor which strives toward perfection, of plant and animal life which proclaims, "I am resplendent still. Already I am become active, avid . . ."

How many times in my life have I benefited from this universal persistence and eagerness? The taste of the sap, the green of the lime tree's bud, the bitterness of the willow twig; each year I have them on my lips. Beneath December's sky, a sucker and its sap, a pollarded tree and its sapwood speak to me of yet another flowering . . .

The commandment to live comes to us from all around, and despite frost, the wheat sprouts and the lime trees redden with a joyous swelling at Christmastime. To sing of spring when it has already arrived would never do for me; I must go to meet it when it first strikes out through the long shadows, feeling its way, venturing into tufts under the arms of the elders, into green ears along the honeysuckle . . . Word of it first comes to me from the provinces it most favors: Brittany has its daphnes, Auray is gathering its violets; a gentler breath has passed over the sea.

Very near Paris, at your feet, that delicate rosette is a young dandelion, and that pearl in its center will one day be its flower. That sort of oblong, incarnadine cherry is the acorn fallen from the oak. It is quite some time since it hurled its seed from itself toward the two greatest adventures—life and death. If the day is calm, the waters free, and the ditches full, you might see sprouting, in green spurs and in tiny valves, the future hyacinth, the lily of the valley about to be . . . The bulbs are stirring. The squill is as blue as an eye. The primose nestles its yellow rosette, and the birds watch the earth soften and steam in the winter sunlight. Some among them have already improvised a little vocal arabesque, a burgeoning melody, with which they promise the world an end to winter and venture a forecast of the season of love.

SNOWDROP

If a bee had three wings, it would be a snowdrop . . .
Or rather, if a snowdrop had but two wings, would it
be a bee? That is how daydreaming goes when it can
escape a painful attack of arthritis and is free to roam.
The little boot of the snowdrop is soaking in a glass of
water nearby, on the banquette table. It is the first one
of the year, but it does not move me nearly as much as
the spur of the first violet, the tip of the hyacinth, or
the bud of the lily of the valley. For the Parisian custom,
butting in where it has no business, is to gather and
assemble the budding snowdrop into bunches, lift its
delicate, closed calix in the air, and paralyze it with no
hope of flowering. How, in this thwarted bouquet, in the
upright, supplicating posture of so many creatures whose
deepest vow is frustrated by the bouquet maker, how

A Nosegay

is one to recognize my three-winged bee, my drooping *pendeloque*, the "pendant earring" of my childhood, with its cinched, green corset, its white skirt unfastened, as early as January, by one gentler breath of air? In Paris they know nothing of its true size or of its secret, of its short, modest underskirt with six scallops and bright, bold, green stripes . . . Does Paris even know that at noon the snowdrop, when free and thriving, exhales the breath of orange blossoms? . . .

I have unbound and put the poor strangled things in water, and I am waiting for them to reassume their normal posture, to nod and shake their heads of tinkling blossoms. It's no use. One or two manage it, then droop and succumb. I will have lessened the strain they were under and allowed them a dignified death.

FLOWER SHOWS

To them, to these imprisoned flowers, I dedicate a portion of that pity that goes out to caged animals. Nearly as alive as they, these flowers die the quicker for having traveled, only to find stingy, shifting, shallow soil. In a plant's withering we can take the measure of how much life it held, and how fast it clung to it. Its drooping and the pathetic bowing of its flower head constitute a genuine faint, accompanied by pallor as the plant suddenly shows the whiter underside of its petals and leaves. If water comes to its rescue in time, it revives in the most moving way. How many moments have I lost—but can I call them lost?—beside such thirsty drinkers as the anemone, the tulip, the hyacinth, the wild orchis! Gasping with heat and thirst, their stems, plunged into water, draw it up so deeply, so greedily, that one can catch the

A Nosegay

flower in an energetic gesture, in its return to the vertical, at first with a jerk, then with successive little twitches, when the top is too lush and too heavy.

It is a sweet thing for a writer to watch a tulip being reborn in a crystal goblet. With the ink on the pen dry, before me still a piece of writing, interrupted by a fleeting death, reaches toward perfection, and will attain it, only to shine one day and founder the next . . . I do better to watch the tulip come back to its senses; I hear the iris unfurl. Its last protective layer of silk rasps and splits along an azure finger, itself unrolled just a short time ago, and sitting alone in a quiet little room, one might be startled if one has forgotten that on a nearby pier table an iris has suddenly decided to bloom. Think of the thousands of irises at Cours-la-Reine, renewed by a continuous flowering. The first light of day delivers those whose time has come, and I begin to long for the moment when, in the canvas-filtered dawn, I can bend an ear toward the audible sigh of so many irises released at once . . .

They bloom without respite even as they suffer, and, with their long canine tongues hanging out—look at the medial nervure, the multiple canals, the fleshy and transparent edge—seem to pant. It is their own perfume suffocating them, so sweet is it, lingering, made for crawling, immediately seconded by that of the petunia. The area where the irises are grouped is a still pool, parted with difficulty by our passage. Excitable women blanch in it, fanning back the unbearable, heavy incense exhaled by so many heraldic tongues, some of which have fur like a leopard's. Whereas among the roses, the ladies lean over not only to smell but to drink as at a fountain. After which these thirsty doves call out to one another and loudly spread the news of a new rose's heretofore unknown fragrance, the more lovely for having gradually complied with the stubborn determination of a gardener who wanted it to look like the poppy, the hollyhock, the flat clematis, the double cherry blossom.

One smells of pampered skin, and the other of blond tobacco, or apricot, or pineapple. But which can compare to the rose that smells of rose? On this one the lips linger and the nostrils throb; one woman who smells it shuts her eyes: "Leave me, I feel as if I have at last arrived in my own land."

A land whose names she would name: Sensuality, Reverie, Literary Affectation, if she could name it. But she knows no more about it than the fact that the scent of the rose is enough to imbue a woman with wordless, sibylline poetry, as if she were younger by ten centuries.

For years we did not give a second thought to the begonia. Emblematic, it found its way into year-end reviews, in which the lobster—the spiny variety—was no match for it. Owing to popular irony, the begonia develops quite strangely. When fully grown and huge, it looks like an exceptional begonia, and then a monstrous begonia. This year we are left stupefied by its megalomaniac flower, which claims to replace the hollyhock, the nasturtium, the poppy, and the rose, all at once. A blaze of incomparable, outrageous colors adorns it; it possesses the most beautifully vibrant reds, a yellow which spills light all around it, and a unique saffron flesh color. But smell it: it has less fragrance than a clump of grass, and touch it, gently: it could not give up its leguminous stiffness or its flesh crisp as a young radish.

I have little regard for these vegetable persons who put on disguises. I am already weary of these exaggeratedly oversized ones. Some breeders make the Brabançon and the fox terrier smaller, others make the Hortensia bigger. Let us be fair to the latter: they admit, even in their shows, that art is not their concern. Here is the blue Hortensia right next to the pink, the blue-violet, then the white, along the lines of kitchen garden geometry. It is enough that each hydrocephalic plant, with its spherical flower upright on its stocky stem, fill out its own bed. One who will be put out by all this is the chrysanthemum.

A touch of romanticism perfumes a rock garden reserved for the bells of the digitalis. They are reminded of their sandy origin, of their thin, burning native soil, scorching the feet of those out walking in July. Their race has known the sun that burns the rocks of Fontainebleau to a cinder, and midday, stifling beneath the tent, cannot make them bend. But a humbler, provincial people, sweet-smelling, drab, delicate, ancient, lies prostrate, in agony at their feet. They bear names that stir my heart: bennet, salvia, potentilla, lupine, cornflower. Who stops for them now? A single gaping gloxinia would gobble them up in one bite. Watch out for the gloxinia! The velvety, fat, expanding newcomer has its eye on the begonia . . . Oh, to be the first to own a gloxinia as big as a slop pail, what a dream!

At noon the little lotus pond exhales, and from the

bottom of its calixes rises the stagnant, soporific odor that puts an end to both activity and appetite. All the other flowers beg for mercy and garden lovers go off to lunch. In the misty, humid, torrid enclosure where the orchids are assembled, "the loveliest of flowers" poses for its portrait. This prized beauty, a cattleya, shows its pedigree and displays itself against a screen of black velvet. A silken bandage is rolled around its foot: as it is for a prized racehorse. Surrounding it there are nothing but blue throats shooting forth a flaming style, wings barely held to a threadlike stem, ophrys and orchis camouflaged as striped fish, as fruit, as bees the color of wine, as hummingbirds: ruses of thinking plants or traps to fool the butterfly, the bird, the insect—and, perhaps, man? What complex design gave shape to the most cunning, the most impenetrable of all, the one that manages to imitate—I'll give you a hundred guesses —the flat and simple corolla, ordinary mauve, and the usual white of the common pansy that thrives in the little gardens of the nuns . . . ?

A Nosegay

FLORA AND FAUNA OF PARIS AND ENVIRONS

"Do you go for a walk every morning?"

"Every morning."

"And what if the weather is bad?"

"Then I walk in bad weather."

"And always in the Bois?"

"Always in the Bois."

Here my interlocutor gave me a perplexed look and added in a general way, "And it doesn't bore you? I would find it deadly boring."

Wherein he was not wrong . . . And I agree that a week or a month of walks in the Bois wouldn't be that amusing.

But I have something like thirty years of the Bois behind me, and that changes everything. In those thirty years the Bois has become familiar and new with each day, as much as a favorite dwelling, the progress of the sun across the wall, the mood of the sea. In an instant, a gust of wind will brush back and change the color of its greenery, my route, the sky, the smell of the well-trod forest floor and the grass. Acacia season does not have the fragrance of lime-tree season; I could never confuse the perfume of the catalpa with that of the bland privet. The satiny trunks of the big wild cherry tree, from which I gather the sapid little berries, do not rise up in the same area as the exotic walnut trees, which in autumn provide me with nuts that are good and hard, with dense meat well defended by a bitter husk that stains the hands. As for mushrooms, I leave it to a specialist to harvest them. He pokes around in the underbrush with a stick as if hunting snakes. He is also the one who un-earths the little wild garlic and with it makes a soup for which he has nothing but praise. I do not know his name, but I know him by sight. He has a dreamy way of speaking about plants, about what the weather is likely to do, and "what goes good with bread . . ." Between two old genii of the woods, one does not ask for more.

What else would you like to know about the flora? Each spring sees the wild cherry, the elder, and the hawthorn perish, blossom by blossom, beneath pillaging hands. I will be careful not to tell you where to find some spindly but very fragrant lilacs free of palisades and gates, or the rose-colored corollas of the quince trees . . . Near Auteuil, there are still some bluebells, as blue as those that April multiplies in the woods of Rambouillet and Fausses-Reposes, but sickly, and besides, Parisians nip all flowers in the bud.

DECEMBER IN THE FIELDS

A rose, white daisies with crimson tips, violets . . . I
gather a May bouquet in December. The mountain bluet
continues to flower and the still-green elm sways . . .
The early Nice spring is no gentler than this Limousin
winter.

"What lovely weather!"

But without a word the gardener points to three
bright stars suspended above the little valley where soon
the sun will set. Already this morning he predicted that
the lower meadow, along the river, will be blanketed
with hoarfrost tomorrow; his gesture summons up the
oracles he does not deign to repeat.

But hoarfrost isn't winter. And snow, if it falls,
can't be called "bad weather" either. "Bad weather" is
an exclusively urban cataclysm, and the city alone experi-

A Nosegay

ences that massive, indisputable phenomenon its inhabitants call winter. Here, amid these living creatures, these plants and animals, there is—brief, varied, renewed by a ray of sun or a gust of wind—mild November, and fickle December, black with rain, white with snow, January bright and crisp; there is a misty yesterday, and a mysterious tomorrow which one awaits, which one discusses while raising a wet finger to the wind . . .

Oh, precious, brief hours of winter days in the country! Summertime belongs to everybody, from its shyest lily of the valley to its first ripe grape, with its unbuttoned raciness, its feasts without secrets. Its name is associated with memories that cheapen it, the words "holiday" and "vacation" . . . With the first fire of autumn, beaten down by the blustery drafts in the fireplace, the smell of damp pine and the long sparks rekindle in us the serious child who once dreamed in front of the fire, over an unread book; the chaste child who has not known love. The deepest, the tenderest memories, those frightened off or made pale by the bright light of happy summers, play discreetly between the fire and the lamp, and perhaps it is not spring, nor its first night, disturbed by too much moonlight or too many nightingales, which best tears from us those disturbing words: "I feel as if I were young again . . ."

Young again—not to know all that one has learned, to stand in amazement, to possess for the first time—wonder attends us, far from these walls. We go to join it, by dipping a hand, and our lips, in the swollen brook tasting of leaves, or else by conquering, at the same time as the sun, a bare countryside, lovely with its stark contours, and from which useless mankind has withdrawn until the sap reawakens. For us, for us alone the pink bramble has flowered again, for us the holly has seeded, and the chilly violet will come to a happy end, by dying on a warm breast, releasing its inimitable soul . . . The gorse flowers three times, fooling a few bees as it does, and the polygonum has no wish to die. So many charms persist on this land some would call stripped! Later it will still have the berry, the russet leaf, the blue spruce, moss in chevrons, in fringe, in furls; it will have everything that might enchant and hold, everything that disdains and turns away from the inconstancy and heedlessness of man who abandons the earth as he does a mistress cherished for her beauty alone, at the moment he fears she might be losing it . . .

A Nosegay

SECRETS

It is now said that they have a complete sensory apparatus, a nervous system, the rudiments of eyes; one part of the scientific world probes in search of their heart, the source, the regulator of the translucid blood that flows through them . . . The greatest learning will once again give way to the greatest anxiety. Uneasiness, qualms, the certainty henceforth of inflicting a real death with every step, remorse at seeing that which we hold to our breast, to our lips, that which we most cherish, falter and succumb at our own hands, is that what we have to look forward to? The screen shows us, in fast motion, the dramas of growth and flowering. We know that corollas manage to blossom only at the price of seemingly conscious efforts; likewise the sticky larva struggles beneath its last shell at the moment the butterfly or the crackling dragonfly unfolds.

Before our very eyes the common sensitive mimosa, in order to throw off any aggressor, bends all its twiggy elbows, lowers its leafy armpits, and surrenders only one swooning trophy. The secrets of plants, their magic defenses fall one by one. Their traps work in the open and reveal the carnivorous instinct, the taste for murder. The glossy edges, rounded into the lip of a lidded chalice, are deadly. Another flower closes interlocking port-cullises of rigid hairs around the insect . . . What! They're cruel, too? They have a demanding sex, a fierce-ness, and fantasies of their own?

It is not impossible that witchcraft, the peasant magic we took for naïve, which gathered simples, distilled sap, and divined flowers, is regaining its prestige. Motion pictures and cinematic enlargements will help it do so by showing the gloxinia and Dutchman's pipe, haunted chasms, the cotyledons of the green bean, spring traps, the bud of the lily, long crocodile jaws yawning for the first time . . . Is that hairy-tongued monster you, my sweet iris? What baleful grimace twists the lip of the rose upon waking! Twenty devil's horns crown the cornflower and the carnation. The climbing pea shoots out a python's head, and the sprouting of a handful of lentils sets in motion an onslaught of hydras . . .

One day, sights such as these, which held me spell-bound in front of the screen, will, I hope, rival the toy train that falls off the bridge into the river, and the arctic debacle charged with carrying off, on its most stable floe, an overweening starlet. Human imaginings

A Nosegay

are short-lived; reality alone can rave on and on without curb or limit: gaze upon the projected and enlarged refractions of precious crystals, architectures of pure light, dizzying perspectives, delirious geometries . . .

I am easily left dumbfounded before such secrets betrayed, the secrets of huge and unrecognizable flowers. And easily do I forget them before a flower in the wild. Our crude eye, freed of overly powerful aids, recovers a traditional poetry. An almanac religion connects us to a flower, even a puny one, when it symbolizes a season, to its color when it commemorates a saint, to its scent if it painfully takes us back to a lost bliss.

In spring, nearly an entire nation demands lily of the valley like bread. Were it not for its fragrance, excessive beyond all logic—I could have written beyond all decency—the lily of the valley would be a meager little flower, bell-shaped and greenish white. It raises itself above the dry leaves at that time of year when the first warm rains fall, heavy drops that free the simple arabesques escaping the blackbird's beak, and the first notes, of a luminous sphericity, springing from the first nightingales . . . I feel my way timidly; I invent a kinship, for which there are no words, among the milky drop from the lilies, the tear of warm rain, and the crystal bubble that rises from the toad . . .

The stirring of spring is so impressive that afterward the advent of the rose is celebrated with less fervor. However, all is permitted the rose—splendor, a conspiracy of perfumes, petalous flesh that tempts the nose, the lips, the teeth . . . And all is said, all is born in the year the moment it arrives; the first rose merely heralds all other roses. How confident it is, and how easy to love! It is riper than fruit, more sensual than cheek or breast. All brushes have painted and will paint it. I have twenty portraits of it, as does everyone. I have her plump, like a cabbage; I have her flat, imitating Persian roses . . .

Here one unknown watercolorist has loaded it down with fluting like a dahlia's, and here an old girl has hollowed it into a little carmine navel. These little paintings of flowers go where I go, modest but enhanced by some arbitrary, mysterious detail, which pleases me like a word whose meaning is half veiled. A rose abounds with them. It is not that I love it more now than in the past, but I strive after it more. I am interested in its prodigious, its inexhaustible talent for metamorphosis, following horticultural fashion. In the gardens of my childhood we picked it huge and unabashedly rose-colored. Holding its head high, it would listen without flagging to the long canticles of the month of Mary and did not faint between two thickets of candles. "Did you see Mme Léger's rose on the altar? Like a head of lettuce, my dear, like a head of lettuce! M. Léger measured it before bringing it to the church, it's eighteen centi-meters in diameter!" Rose roses, blue larkspurs turned red by some mysterious oxidation; you, black roses, a preserve of scent, I loved you enough to watch you change as I myself was changing. Does anyone bother anymore to champion the cabbage rose, with its Second Empire skirt? As for the larkspur, it reigns, twenty times bigger, under the name delphinium . . . You can still see the black rose in its native province. Cheek to cheek, the one pale, the other black and scarlet as sin, a lone woman and an inexhaustible flower intoxicate one another . . .

Twenty-five years ago, at an old man's nursery in Besançon, chance brought me face to face with the rosebush that bears edible fruit. Its rough, grainy leaves, whispering in the wind, and its red eglantine were less striking than its regular fruit, with a little pomegranate crest, sourish, with a delicate, candied aftertaste. The old man died, as did his rosebush, and I spoke of them hundreds of times, and hundreds of times I asked in vain, "Can anyone tell me where there still grows a rosebush with edible fruit?" I have enlarged it in my memory, I would depict it with fire and without hope, as one does a lover perfected in death.

And then, just the other day at Versailles, in a painstakingly disheveled American garden, I noticed that I was walking between two hedges of edible-fruit-bearing roses, dense, pruned back, treated like box and yew . . . "Very good for enclosures," the ultrawealthy amateur of humble gardens instructed me. Then he led me toward his rose garden, and I came in contact with what pretended to be even newer: nasturtium-colored roses that smelled like peaches; flimsy roses, and of a dirty mauve, that smelled of crushed ants; orange roses that did not smell at all; lastly, a little horror of a rosebush with yellowish flowerets, fuzzy, misshapen, bushy, responsible for an unpleasant menagerie of musky smells, the smells of a gymnasium used exclusively by red-headed young women, and of artificial vanilla, a plant the amateur called by the name "rose," without my having the courage to appeal, other than with my eyes, to those sovereigns white as snow, dark as blood, apricot-plum, pale on the outside, flushed deep in their heart, consecrated by universal homage . . .

Rose, increased in size, shrunk, perverted, disguised, docile in the fickle hands of men, you can still arouse and calm what remains in us of love's folly. Rose, I consent to your being the final blaze around which the meditative circle of old lovers assembles. If they sigh, seized by the spring stirring, "I'm trembling with cold," rest assured that more than one is listening inside himself and holding back the long confession from the past: "I'm shivering with morning, with March, with flight, with faceless hope, with seeds, with forgetting . . . I'm trembling with hyacinths, with hawthorn, with tears . . ."

A Nosegay

REDOUTÉ'S ROSES

That poetry should issue from a faithful rendering, respectful of its model, one in which the imagination reserves no portion for itself, is quite a rare occurrence, and one which remains a thing of wonder. It repays the painter more often than the writer, for whom success is less a matter of thought than of a coming together of words. When called upon, signs floating through the air, words sometimes deign to descend, gather, and arrange themselves . . . So it is that the small miracle I call the golden egg, the bubble, the flower seems to take shape: a sentence worthy of what it set out to describe.

Faced with his task, all the more thankless because better known to him and for a longer time, the writer envies the painter. But if he holds nature too close, if he does not tear himself away from the lesser art of "making likenesses," the painter laments over having missed his poetic calling, which is to win the viewer over to an arbitrary truth.

Redouté was untroubled by noble and lyrical deviation. Coming at the age of lovely, painstaking entomologies, obliged, moreover, to teach his art to princesses exempt from genius, Redouté manifests a love for flowers that has no fear of exhausting its subject. Knowing that nature does not repeat itself, and that a newborn rose is never the rebeginning of a rose that is dead and gone, he serenely painted dynasties of roses. "Not quite different, not quite the same," each of Redouté's roses lays claim to strictly generic qualities, according to which it unfurls its petals, bedecks its long sepals with little bristles, multiplies its red family of stamens, assumes an ovoid shape before blooming, lowers its head earthward or tilts it back in bliss, bristles with curved thorns, irrigated with rose-colored blood, or reduces its defenses to a mossy sheath . . . Sisters, not twins, on first sight, Redouté's roses inspire likes and preferences—how could one confuse them? Each has its own name, and even its own jewels. The painter has not given all of them the cabochon of dew, or the little Argus butterfly, azure here, bronze there, the magnificent Painted Beauty with its half-moons, or some rounded insect whose hard chitin sparkles . . .

Botanical learning, which burst forth from Redouté, helped him to establish a style, to heighten a floral attitude with authority. Over the years, this scrupulousness loses its documentary modesty. Today, in all the plates chosen for this album, what the artist intended as instruction becomes the lyricism of exactitude, and demands our enthusiasm in the name of the present. The science of depicting white on white, of faithfully reproducing the intricacy, the density, the bristling heart, the horned pistils, is here deferential and complete. In the camellia gallery the "fat" of the flesh and the glossiness of its hardy foliage touch us as only the certainty, the sensuality of a vigorous life touches us, recorded by a calm artistry whose grace is perhaps not always an act of will.

Well after Redouté scientific curiosity carried the pursuit of plant sensibility much farther. A system of veins and nerves, pulses, and voluntary movements appear in plants. Beneath the lenticular eye the secrets of the flower fall one by one, and we happen upon the subterranean course of its roots, their headlong or tentative choices. We know that germination is an onslaught of hydras, and the yawning of the cotyledons a voracious reflex . . . Discovering what formerly had been hidden from him is the headiness, the honor, and the downfall of man. Peaceful horticulture itself grows enflamed by wanting more, and better, and too much. If mere enlargement must be taken as progress, today we record many a case of gigantism, a sort of flower abuse which turns the gloxinia into an abyss, the throat of the gladiolus into a red crater, and soon will toast to the morning glory's goblet. We have already gotten a little blasé about all this. What amazement, what pleasure we do experience comes from what we have forgotten. Open Redouté: how slight the Greater Clematis was back then in Marie Antoinette's gardens. And this tiny, ugly little thing, this yellowish color coiffed, provincial-style, with two small purple bands, such was the pansy, which nowadays opens the wide, dark wings of a moth . . . If Redouté were to come back and still wished to paint this little pansy, he would have to search among the rocks for the garden exile, in poorer soil with its neighbor the mignonette, wild like her, and provided like her with an unsettled and delicate scent . . .

These botanical portraits, books of images devoted to flowers and fruit, the last and rarest copies of these grand pomologies still intact—which the decorative mind tears apart and scatters, framed, on walls—are sought after by the collector, who locks them away, for all passions are jealous and dream of lock and key. *Les Roses* is still around, in small numbers; some of Redouté's other flowers once again come to light. The plates that accompany the text, and which alone count toward the glory of such a collection, derive from an art which, thank God, still depends entirely on the hand of man. In color lithography, everything is human discernment, skill, and decision. It is a wonder these days that an art that has not evolved still lovingly uses age-old tools that die in its service. At Mourlot Brothers, inside their old and majestic building, I read on one of the presses its age: 1870—and it is not the oldest of the laborers, bathed in shadow, that project the first transparent yellow on a field of beautiful paper, delicately and almost imperceptibly bistre, out of which the ruff of a narcissus, the petal of a buttercup, the surface of dappled foliage will take shape. A shade of pale green, a little like the color of a jonquil, comes next, and already the style and the size

A Nosegay

of the future bouquet can be made out. The second green, bluer than the first, which comes next, traces the venation, a fine covering of hairs, the tuft of stamens, and immediately precedes the application of the rose color . . . One cannot look upon the successive stages of a color lithograph without some feeling of tenderness.

Twelve, fourteen lithographic stones; twelve, fourteen colors are used to bring a single plate of Redouté's to life. The appearance of the first rose ink lights up the entire plate, situates the petals, signifies the arrival of a sanguine life, primes the curved thorn and the closed bud. Then the violet and the blues will be the forecolors of the crimson red, which crowns a piece of work caressed by conscious hands, on a series of stones whose grain itself is a matter of choice—I was going to write of vintage, so well known is their provenance and consistent their quality.

Every emergence entails, demands its share of love. I was not aware of the passing of time, which flows with the sound of a motorboat, among the Mourlot Brothers and their co-workers. Oh, endless Paris! These, the last of their kind, bear on their faces the variety, the refinement that is theirs for living in a murderous and magnificent city, in the practice of a trade in which the eye does not risk losing its taste for color, its critical sense. In the space of one week, they handle, trace, place on the stone, and pull Rouault, Redouté, or an advertisement. One of the doyens, graying somewhat, has a wild head of hair, and in his direct, caustic gaze a fire that is Paris's alone. If I were a painter, I would love to paint this artist-artisan, bending over the peaceful sensuality of a

Redouté rose. At his side rests an old press, whose big wooden wheel, polished and mellowed with use, is shaped like a motionless star . . .

A Nosegay

THE LIFE AND DEATH OF THE PHYLLOCACTUS

"Suddenly this morning my phyllocactus made up its mind to flower. As ephemeral as its flower is, I hope it will last the day and that this descendant of Sido's rose cactus will not take leave of the world till nightfall . . ."

To say ephemeral is not enough. Born of the morning, this wondrous flower has already begun to die. I will not leave its side before its final gasp. André Barbier had it brought to me an hour ago.

Thanks be to thee once more, Sido, my mother, you who chose this spectacle above all others—the blossoming of the rose cactus! Had you not written a certain brief letter, which I stuck into *Break of Day*, I would not be here gazing as you did upon the fatal and swift miracle of this flowering and its undoing in the bright, declining light of June, before a dry little pot, before a plant the shape of an ugly green lath which invests all its pride, all its quick fate, in a single bloom, a single explosion long promised and for a long time deferred.

It is . . . no, it was, an hour ago, of a whiteness as pure as the water lily's. Already, a darkening is creeping over it. But I can still call it white, still celebrate a shade of white on its long petals which crowns neither the gardenia nor the magnolia nor the lily. A viridescent mystery, barely visible, begins at the base of its calix and slowly spreads throughout . . . Leaning over it, can I write, can I even think the word "slowly"? We are speaking of an instant, of the time it takes to sigh. What was thrust forth fails, what was brandished surrenders, but glory and arrogance find refuge in the heart of the corolla, where they are still assured white's protection. Long, long petals, as long as a small hand, a lovely spatulate shape—each spatula ending in a harmless spine —a unanimous coalition around a hearth of stamens, around the most vulnerable point . . . But I had still to discover the center of the center: a single scape rises up and rips its own peak open into a star, reminding one of a starfish, a yawning sea cucumber, a sea anemone unfurled at the tip of its stem, a geometric crystal of snow . . . We are quick to look, to compare—but to what end? Some powerful and insidious thing comes and attacks a flowery section of the corolla, which yields. The inseparable brown and green of all corruption conquers the creature that waited four years for its one day of recompense.

"Deflowered it will go to the museum," writes André Barbier, "which will take good care of it."

A Nosegay

Another long sleep awaits it. Or perhaps its exertions have taken it beyond that repose from which we hope to recall it. What does it matter, since in a single day it has accomplished and celebrated a passionate season all its own?

FLORA

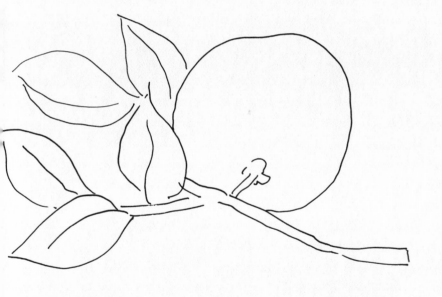

AND POMONA

FLORA AND POMONA

"Let's give the young mimosas a little something to drink," I said to my gardener in Provence.

For the fire in the sky was sapping the life out of my transplanted "four seasons," and their oblong leaves, which resemble the leaves of the olive tree, were parched and limp.

But my gardener shook her head. "They got water yesterday. They're not getting any more till tomorrow."

"But look at them! They're thirsty!"

My gardener raised her arms. "Well, to hear them tell it, they never get a drop! The more you give them, the more they ask you for. It's bad enough that whenever I want to water those tomatoes I planted next to them, I have to do it on the sly."

Any more and she would have threatened them

with punishment, as she did her own strict private life, accused of "striking noon" around eleven-thirty just to get its meal earlier. When it came to rooted creatures, she could upset me quite easily by talking like a sooth-sayer or a bonesetter. Lowering her voice, she said, "They droop like that on purpose," and motioned to-ward the "four seasons'" mimesis. I was and always have been only too ready to call what is—perhaps—a merely automatic reflex fakery and sentiment when faced with a plant's faints and revivals, its abrupt turns toward the light, its keenness to live as well as to kill. Contrary to what I had at first hoped, the enlargements brought to life on the screen—a gross miracle, the biggest of photography's indiscretions—have left me rather cold, as if the role of photographic exactitude were at times to violate the truth by enlarging it, and to deceive the human eye, to inebriate it with speeded-up or slow motion. To lie about a creature's rhythm is very near to lying about its essence. I have experienced the anguish and the joy of perceiving life in the plant king-dom not at the movies but through my feeble though complete senses, each shored up by the other, not by overloading or wildly exaggerating what my eyes see.

Like many who have lived close to the gentle vege-table world, I know its benevolence, and I rebel against an artificial rhythm that transforms germination and growth into onslaughts and blossoming into the yawning of wild beasts: the gloxinia into a trap, the lily into a crocodile, and string beans into hydras. If you expect me to accept the gigantization of the cinema, then along with it you must give me the plant's din, in synchrony and as an equal lie; increase a thousand times, too, the thunder of flowerings, the cannonade of exploding pods, and the ballistics of seeds. The plant world is not mute, though the sound of its activity reaches us only by chance, as an exception, as a subtle recompense accorded either our vigilance or our laziness, which, by the fruit it bears, is worth as much as the closest observation.

At Cours-la-Reine I loved to visit the flower shows that so faithfully marked out the year. First came the azaleas, then the irises and the hydrangeas, the orchids, and, last of all, the chrysanthemums. I can recall an extraordinary profusion of irises in May . . . Thousands upon thousands of irises, a mass of azure bordering on a mass of yellow, a velvety blue-violet confronted with a pale, pale mauve, black irises the color of spiderwebs, white irises with the sweet smell of iris, irises blue as a nocturnal storm, and Japanese irises with long tongues . . . There were tiger flowers, too, with their magnificent, showy rags, like a saltimbank's . . . Thousands upon thousands of irises, busy being born and dying, punctually, ceaselessly, busy mingling their fragrance with the fetid odor of some mysterious fertilizer . . .

As noisy as our Paris was in those days, it always had its unexpected moments of stillness. At Cours-la-Reine, between one and one-thirty in the afternoon, when the last trucks had reached their canteens, those who loved flowers and silence could savor a strange respite, a solitude in which the flowers seemed to recover from human curiosity. The heat filtered by the canvas roof, the absence of any breeze, the heavy, sleepy air charged with scent and humidity, these are goods that Paris is in the habit of hoarding. Peace reigned, but not silence, which was disturbed by a faint, insistent sound, more delicate than the nibbling one hears in a silkworm nursery, a sound of scratched silk . . . The sound of wing cases opening, the sound of tiny insect feet, the sound of dead leaves dancing was irises, in the soft, conducive light, loosening the dry membrane rolled up at the base of their calices, irises opening by the thousands.

The rasping sound of a very real existence, a very real exigency, the thrust of the bud, the twitching erection of a bloodless stem just given its liquid nourishment, the greediness of water-logged stems like the hyacinth's, the tulip's, the daffodil's, the fantastic growth of the mushroom, which rises up while brandishing on its round cap the leaf that witnessed its birth—these are the spectacles and the music I came to respect more and more as my curiosity grew. Is this to say that I handle the feelings, the sufferings of plants with kid gloves, out of scrupulousness or compassion; that I fret over cutting into the fiber, lopping off the head, or drying up the sap? No. Deeper love does not mean greater pity.

All of us wince when a rose, falling apart in a tepid room, lets go of one of its shell-like petals and sends it adrift into its own reflection on a smooth, marble surface. The sound of its fall, very soft, distinct, is like a syllable of silence, and enough to move a poet. The peony loses its petals all at once, in a wheel around the base of its vase. But I don't go in for the spectacles and symbols of a graceful death. Speak to me instead of the triumphant sigh of irises in travail, of the arum which creaks as it unrolls its cornet, of the big scarlet poppy which forces open its green, slightly hairy sepals with a little *cloc*, then hastens to stretch out its red silk beneath its sprouting seed capsule covered with a good crop of blue stamens! Nor is the fuchsia mute. Its reddish bud does not open its four shutters, or raise them like pagoda horns, without a faint smacking of lips, after which it frees its charming, rumpled petticoat of white, pink, or purple . . . In its presence, in the presence of the morning glory, how can one not conjure up other births, the great imperceptible din of the broken chrysalis, the moist, folded wing, the first leg feeling its way into an unfamiliar world, the fairy eye whose facets receive the shock of the first earthly image? . . . The death scene of a corolla leaves me cold. But a flower at its debut thrills me, as does the start of a long, lepidopterous career. Where is the majesty in that which is ending, alongside the unsteady departures, the disorders of dawn?

Defense, attack, struggle for survival, and victory: in our climate we are spared the worst battles engaged in by large and devouring exotic plants, yet here the sweet little butterwort rolls its hairy leaf around the insect and digests it, and the pipe of the Aristolochia fills with tiny victims. If its appetite makes a plant resemble an animal, I like it no more than I like an animal that resembles a human. "Wouldn't you like me to give you a little monkey?" someone once asked me. "No, thank you," I replied, "I'd prefer an animal." I cast out all trap flowers, with their busy mandibles and their deadly secretions. So many crimes perpetrated by one kingdom on another! Oh, lovely pink chestnut tree, shall I not once again this spring have to free the bee caught in the varnish of your sticky bud? But at least you are lovely. And what is one to think, to the shame of all lords and ladies, of a certain arum? . . . Its phallic spike surrounds it with the stench of rotting meat, which fools and intoxicates clouds of insects. They hurl themselves into a drunken stupor, clustered and heaped together inside the cornet, fighting over everything it dispenses, death included, and, once prostrate, forget their antagonism. In my horror, I would like to know . . .

No, I would not like to know. Let the small black secret remain crouching in the depths of the flower-of-evil-haunts. A lot of good it does to define, name, or foresee what ignorance lets me look upon as wondrous! Neither the flower nor its influence can be explained. Is it shape and coloring that make certain leaves marvelous? Our question applies as well to its modest flower. One adolescent boy lost a good deal of his admiration for bougainvillea, that mantle of orange, violet, and pink fire that covers Algerian walls. "Now that I know they're only bracts . . ." he said, without further explanation.

Oh yes, only bracts. We would revere none but the vessel, none but the flower.

Lord knows how I admire the walled orchards on the gentle lands of the Ile-de-France. Worked and re-worked, loosened and tormented by man and enriched by him, there is not an inch of certain choice districts that has not borne cherry or pear, currant or raspberry. The goblet-shaped pruning puts the fruit within hand's reach and hollows out the tree so that air and sunlight can reach inside. Who should win the prize among the raspberry misted over with a mauve pruinescence, the Montmorency cherry with skin so fine that the pit shows through it against the light, and the mirabelle plum stippled like a cheek? Yet a fruit tree's glory, the most lasting image it leaves us, the one we look back on most passionately, is the memory of its ephemeral flowering. The white sleeves slipped over the arms of the cherry trees, the early green-white stars of the plum trees, the pear trees' creamy white bristling with brown stamens, and finally, the apple trees white as roses, rosy as snow at dawn—that froth, those swans, those phantoms, those angels are born, billow, disappear, and die scattered. But those seven days blot out the more solid splendor, the durable and joyous season of fruit. Hand filled and hefting a big, long pear, we say, "Do you remember the day the pear trees on this hill all blossomed at once?"

Because, though modest and small, and without much color, a blossom has all the qualities of an explosion, whereas, once put forth, the leaf has no choice but to grow. What a beauty the caladium, and its big, boat-shaped leaf flooded with pink, green, and brown! Yet it is no more than a big leaf after having been a little leaf. Between bud and bloom there takes place a miracle of effort, then of efflorescence. The flower alone has its sex, its secret, its climax. After it, even the hail from the convulsive seed of the balsam and the crackling pod of the ripe furze have less mystery about them.

How long have men been giving their lives in

return for a plant? A flower, all for a flower. And for it the mountain climber is killed as he reaches for the gentian, the alpine rose, the edelweiss. The explorers of another hemisphere—call them Marcoy, Charnay, or Harmand—traverse South America, from ocean to ocean, come face to face with Mexico . . . For a flower? No, but they run into floral enticements they had not believed to be so potent. There fever grips them, releases them, and grips them again; blue and green snakes dangle overhead, and wild animals draw up short, startled before the white man. Yet the man gathers orchids, sits down on a little camp stool, at the crossroads of four or five mortal dangers, and, between two hurricanes, sketches an orchis and its full complement of petals, antennae, tongues, lunulae, and numbers, before the onslaught of invincible ants . . . One of my heroes, lying in wait on a jaguar path, looked up and saw an unfamiliar flower. Thus spurned, the jaguar passed by, fresh enough and flowered with spots enough to rival the *Oncidium papilo* which the hunter had just picked over him . . . Coming to a halt, the man of science, a dumbstruck child, forgot about his empty stomach, his aching feet, the huge mosquitoes, and the scorpions, to administer first aid to his half-dead plant. He laid it out and fixed it in his herbarium, where it became cumbersome, as do all cadavers . . .

I read and reread, respectfully and amusedly, the memorable voyages of these poor men. Nearly penniless, with three worn-out mules, a few rifles, a handful of Negroes, some glass beads, and . . . the herbarium. It was the herbarium that a man, swimming with one arm, held above the rapids—the herbarium that was covered with ponchos and palm fronds to protect it from tropical downpours, it that was locked inside a tin trunk because of termites . . . Eventually the herbarium made it as far as a museum and fell into a slumber in some provincial hypogeum, a dissected, sterilized wonder, thinner than a potato chip, flat and unrecognizable, looking like nothing that had ever been alive. And our good man, our jungle rover, ever humble and brave, did his utmost to bring it back to life. "You see, in the wild, this part of the plant is an indescribable rosy flesh color, speckled with crimson . . . Here the flower sends out from its corolla an aerial aigrette of stamens, a rostrum of the most beautiful yellow gold . . . Naturally, you can't tell anymore . . . As for its scent, so sweet, so overpowering, that it holds sleep at bay . . . Nights in those latitudes . . ." And he broke off the impossible description with a gesture of futility . . .

Still, he knew how to speak of what he loved, and even to write rather well, this man who traveled to the antipodes, without the aid of motion pictures or telephony, with or without wires, who got it into his head to travel up the Zambezi and the Amazon, to unlock the secrets of the Mato Grosso, and to carry back between his shirt and his heart a bulb inaccessible until then. In addition to the names I have already mentioned, he was also called Baker and Serpa Pinto. He had, if not strange sideburns, a beard your eyes would not believe and hair like a lion's mane, which, he claimed, protected him from both the rays of the sun and the dew of tropical nights. Innocently, he took with him from Europe his favorite dogs—water spaniels, and even English bulldogs—then wept to see them die, nearly roasted alive in the 120° heat. He knew how to do without, but carried his bourgeois revulsion with him and could not get used to the native foods, to a cereal that might have cured his dysentery. It was this brave heart, this pure soul, this child, this finicky little Frenchman, he and no other, who went off to gather flowers in swamps more ghostly than a nightmare, armed with a single cure-all: one kilo of quinine . . .

Today I entrust myself to none but this man when I want to roam the world without leaving my armchair. With him I hunt the lion, I rescue a hummingbird caught in the jaws of two huge, ferocious ants, and, out on some gigantic limb, between a fasting python and a nest of mason wasps, I make a delicate conquest of the extravagant Oncidium of Galeotti.

Is this to say that I, like him, am particularly fond of the orchid kind? Not at all. In vain does it display its red antennae, cover itself with arabesques the color of dried blood, and show off all its glamour on an abdomen-pedestal, fat and purple as a Monsieur plum. And it avails another floral sprite of the funereal swamps nothing at all to appear in the guise of a pale-pink fairy, all got up in gauzy linen, for in such exotic company I would soon be sighing for a rose. But my feverish, my errant guide with scorched feet stalks the wild orchid, and I follow. He makes his way full of faith, with a parrot on his shoulder, a trusty little goat he took in, and a kangaroo of tender years in a leather pouch hanging from a staff. Ecstatic, he murmurs

Flora and Pomona

botanical litanies: "Ah, it's *Aristolochia labiosa*, it's *Trichopilia tortilis* . . ." The only thing I have against him is that he teaches me Latin vocables when it is common names I wish to know. But with what familiar names is one to dub creatures mad with mimicry, disguised as birds, hymenoptera, gaping wounds, and sexual organs? The Aristolochia has a duck's bill, a rash-like pestilence which manifests itself in violet on a whitish background, and a full Spanish petticoat which hangs down to its heels and leaves the stench of a corpse in its wake. The *Miltonia* is put together out of geographical bits and pieces, continents of bronzed gold on yellow seas. The same holds for Oncidium, for Stanhopea, and for *Trichopilia*. And I allow my guide his supreme mirage: his home, where he intends to set down, miraculously safe, like his own pale, anemic self, the unique flower, the precious bulb, the poor, shivering little monster—the remains of the volant orchid, torn from the dark continent.

Creating a garden takes us back to childhood imaginings. As we lose our childhood, we lose a large part of the gift of invention. Only yesterday's gardens were genuine creations, despite their seeming naïveté, their cramped quarters planted with the heads of marigolds, carrot tops, and hawthorn berries, and encircled by a tiny river whose sand was forever drinking up whatever we poured on it from our little watering can. Every child has devised a garden to his own liking. My second brother used to put up tombstones for dolls, and steles the size of a shrew mouse, among which his soul would wander where none could read. Somewhat simpler, I from a very young age abhorred straight, tree-lined paths and four-sided gardens. I wanted them bounded by curves, always bordering the side of a hill or the edge of a wood, facing south or west. No creature changes so much that one cannot recognize, in the comfortable surroundings of her adulthood, the improvisational élan of a little girl—with a wheelbarrow for a prop—that would spring up in a corner of the kitchen garden or beneath the thick cover of the yews.

Many a garden has left its memory with me. Nearly all were to my liking, except those that were too young or that were up to me to plant. It's all well and good to espalier a wall, to mend the palmettes and cordons. But if I am the one who puts the so-called ornamental tree into the ground, it's too slow and I'm too quick. I no longer have the time to wait for its lovely top, its round shadow, or its dense tangle of branches. The oak, the beech, and all meditative varieties of trees take a generation. In the autumn of our years, we can still deal gaily with flowering shrubs or divert ourselves with weigela, the snowy deutzia, a humble diet of syringa and robinia, and the old wig sumac, cloud clad and iridescent in the morning mist.

I did not learn the art of horticulture from my sedentary childhood and adolescence, confined within the bounds of two or three cantons. The neighboring châteaux knew little more than I, because for a long time no one had even dreamed of rejuvenating or scrambling the design of their grounds, generally Louis XIV, redone by the Second Empire. In the center of their lawns, in front of the terrace with its scaly lions, stood the three-tiered compote dish that provided the water for the basin and its goldfish. Around it there still were flower beds in the French style, impoverished by habit and time. An air of kinship hovered over the greenery of these country estates, and with good cause. The gardener of the château at Saint-Sauveur would provide seedlings to the Jeannets, who then shared cuttings and seeds with the house at Orme-du-Pont, whose steward in turn made the Barrès' parterres bloom . . . Now and then a younger and less casual gardener would draw interlaced letters or a coat of arms with dwarf plants on the grassy slope supporting the terrace and try to resuscitate some very old boxed orange trees by giving them a good pruning.

On Sundays, our childhood and adolescent outings, part pleasure, part obligation, would have as destination one of the local manor houses protected only by open gates, some overgrown ha-has, and walls held together by ivy and cemented with thick, velvety moss. We never overstepped these bounds. The presence and the reputation of a few old families, a little uppity and stay-at-homish, faithful attendants at High Mass, were enough to bar the way. In small bands of little girls feigning boldness, we would get as far as a tree-lined walk whose cavernous majesty left us speechless. A few steps more, then a side path bastioned with old lilac bushes, guelder roses, and altheas, and the château, un-veiled and naked, would shimmer in the four o'clock sun.

The loud, bell-like barking of the pointers in the kennel would give us away, but no hand pushed open the tall, half-closed shutters or grabbed hold of the handles of the wheelbarrow abandoned at the foot of the stairs. And the only ones who came to meet us were the slow-moving fragrances delegated by the peppery yellow rosebush, the blossoming lime trees, and the big scarlet poppy whose stem is as bristly as a wild boar and which is secretly wounded at the base of its corolla with the black and blue mark of a bruise.

Silence embroidered with the over-and-over of the bees and the tree frogs, a warmth trapped beneath the dense hedgerows, a huffy storm kept at a respectful distance behind the hills, the distant treadle of a wheat thresher—such today are still the raw materials from which I am able to re-create summer, as if the summer months, independent of hot weather and lazy beaches, were given over to the power of a certain slowing of time, reserved for the provinces of central France, anxious to remain hidden there, settled in and surrounded by espaliers. I see a Téton-de-Vénus peach, still slightly green, already somewhat pink, nibbled and abandoned on the path by the little teeth of the dormouse that picked it; it is summer I see. Are the windows of a modest manor open wide onto dark rooms, their muslin curtains puffed outdoors by the breeze? That is summer. And summer, decanted in ritual responses exchanged by the ladies of the village, who marked Sunday by opening their parasols; summer in the long-ago names of the strawberries—pink hautboys, June beauties, Haquin-de-Liège; this last one very ugly, which upon ripening turned a dark shade of cyanic blue, musky as a tropical fruit, which never made it from the garden to the table without being bruised, bleeding and staining the basket and the tablecloth . . . There you are, summer, and in your August your guests who can't bear the sun . . . In the shade you assign places to the children of the château and their parents behind the shutters, around a nicely laid tea . . . But the dining room is icy and the children sneeze. Between the leaden galette and the pound cake there sits enthroned a cantaloupe, mysterious as a well, which has drunk a whole glass of port and two teaspoons of sugar . . . Outside, when tea is over, the sun has changed place and the frogs are singing . . . O Summer, my desert . . .

Once, sticking my nose between two bars of an iron gate, I saw at the edge of the central lawn a woman enlarged by a white smock and an old straw hat who, bending with difficulty, was bundling up freshly clipped suckers from the rosebushes. A tall, thin man followed her with his eyes, and when he took off his hat to wipe his forehead, I recognized, by his silvery white hair, the lord of the manor.

"Time to rest, Yolande," he called out. "You know what happens when you overdo it!"

The besmocked bundler said something in reply which I couldn't hear, yet I blushed to have caught in the humblest intimacy a couple who never let themselves be seen at Sunday Mass any way but upright, in their armor of taffeta and starch, apportioning what was left of their youth over the distance between the footboard of their carriage and the church pew marked with a crown.

At all times, the Frenchman, while living off the land for economy's sake, has realized that the cultivation of flowers and the care it demands are extravagant uses of time and money. He limits his horticultural luxuries to the hardier rosebushes, the obliging lilac, the red hawthorn—and still he accuses the last of "bringing the caterpillars with it." The villager in love with his garden immediately becomes a "character." The chief town of my district had its own rose man, whose old tortoise mouth held the stem of a rose from one year's end to the next. In winter he kept a whole harem of potted roses warm indoors. The gloxinia appeared very late where we lived and caused several rivalries. It did not overthrow the big "caterpillar," the sleeve of blue-violet campanula that grows immoderately, framing the windows in a single rush and decking them with flowers all season long.

The Breton manor house has its big arborescent lotus, its broom, even its mimosas and its grand, star-shaped paths leading up to it, planted with sextuple rows of trees, its dense ramparts of firs perfectly even and without a breach. Inhospitable by nature, a Frenchman tends his immediate surroundings in a defensive manner, encircles himself with wild rosebushes, blackthorn, and juniper; if necessary, he barbs his garden, and his first flight of fancy tends toward enclosures. In the Midi, the land merchant has invented a temptation for the buyer. He surrounds the subdivisions of his plot with a low wall, which he then tops off with a palisade. And reassured, having gotten the feel for "his place" from the gate and its lock, the new owner, pressing his smile against his grillework, showing a little tooth, there, on his plot of land, takes the measure of a meridional garden.

Flora and Pomona

With the help of time, the garden of the house I grew up in lost the knack for keeping out intruders. All I knew of it was a harmless gate, open day and night. The whole village knew how to shake the carriage gate's big door so as to dislodge a heavy iron bar on the other side that should have bolted it shut. The final instructions, at lights-out, went against common sense: "Be sure not to shut the door onto the stoop, one of the cats isn't back yet! Is the hayloft door open at least? If not, that tomcat will come miaowing outside my window for me to let him in at three in the morning!"

Upper Garden, Lower Garden (the names say enough about the unevenness of the ground) allowed us to slip out unnoticed, once the wall was scaled, and, unnoticed, to slip back in. Both of them, mixing the useful and the superfluous, put the tomatoes and the eggplants at the foot of the pyrethrums and planted lettuce between the impatiens and the heliotropes. If our Hortensias were regally puffed up with pink crowns, it was not because of any particular care but because they were almost touching the pump, thus benefiting whenever the last drops from the watering can were flung through the air and the pitchers were rinsed, and so drank to their heart's content. What more did our garden's reputation need than an indefatigable hundred-year-old honeysuckle, than the cascading wistaria and the nymph's-thigh rose? From these three, climbing and loosening the iron railing, twisting a gutter and creeping under the slate tiles of a roof, I learned what is meant by profusion, by cloying perfumes and their surfeit of sweetness.

Everyone creates in his own image. My friends will

tell you that I do not design gracefully spare, thinly sown gardens. I like a big flowery bundle that suddenly bars the garden path and blocks the view. I don't like glorious landscapes entering my house through every door and window at all hours of the day and night. To every deserving tree I will give air and room, without delay, and as if I myself were dying of suffocation. But the disorderliness in the gardens I cared for was never what it seemed. A certain disarray can be managed only in collaboration with the pruning shears.

My astonished eyes have seen one of Blasco-Ibáñez's gardens, furnished with benches of solid faience, on which, against a white background, could be seen all manner of enameled fruit—apples, apricots, oranges, and pears. A monumental orchard, funereal enamel fruits to break the teeth of the quick and the dead—benches to rest on as soft and inviting, indeed, as a Spanish bed of state.

The gardens of our native France do not greatly benefit from long hours of planning and deep thought. I have never set eyes on the gardens of Claude Monet, but I know that at times he wanted them blue and at others pink. Among those prospects, whose magnificence he alone had orchestrated, he would go about, looking like himself, dressed in a full, bright garment, and I recall that my cheeky youth made a shocking judgment of the handsome, immutable host of those changing Edens, in the sense that I would have wished to see the master of the gardens decline or grow green again, somber and vermilion by turns, according to his mood and age, amid seasons and plants taken out from under the tyranny of his artistry. But perhaps I was misinformed about Monet and his flower governing . . . ?

On the other hand, I like the remark made by a Frenchwoman who had returned from a lengthy stay in lands whose gloomy exuberance knows almost no variation: "One can do without spring, if one must. But not to have autumn, well really, that was more than I could bear." A singular remark, one which makes it seem we might expect more from the annual demise than from the first fruits. As a most likable illiterate, a lover of gardens and of all things that live, fail, and thrive put it: "What do you expect, there's got to be bad weather!"

Born forty kilometers from Paris, about my age, he could neither read nor write. When I showed my astonishment, he simply said, "It just didn't turn out that way."

"But there's a law that makes it mandatory . . ."

At these words, he turned his gaze toward the deep and dense horizon that had protected him from the truant officer and the schoolmaster: the forest of Rambouillet began at my door and seemed to go on forever, a beautiful state preserve of which I knew only the most well-beaten and well-lit paths, the routes leading to the Dutch Ponds' lily of the valley, to the bluebells of Gros-Rouvre, to the wood anemones of Les Mesnuls, and to the big red foxgloves of the groves beyond Saint-Léger . . .

But, for my likable illiterate, the forest did not abound in flowers alone. A home, a refuge, a school, a book in which learning for him was alive, pure and crystal clear, written in sunlight and rain—he got everything from the forest and had never left its nests, its groves, its game . . . A slight man, for all that, whose frailty had, he confided to me, obliged him to marry and to live with a roof over his head. Late in life, he worked as a day gardener for Parisians who had cut into the forest's edge and built their flimsy houses there. He hardly did any work at all in my garden. I wasted all his time drawing on the sure, unfaltering memory of a creature untroubled and unencumbered by the typed page or the printed word. How poor I felt whenever he spoke! In his mouth the names of birds, trees, and grasses, and tales from the woods, would fit their objects like the bee fits the flower. A certain kindheartedness—I was going to say saintliness—turned him away from poaching and nest-robbing. Poachers are oftentimes quite shrewd, and they interest me. They are full of information when they are in a storytelling mood. But something in their silence makes me keep my distance. Their silence has listened once too often to the last sounds of the last terrors which raise feathers, contract the flesh, and glaze the soft eyes of captive animals with a bluish film.

With the light shed by my sapient illiterate, I tried to illuminate the darkness I find myself in when it comes to birds. But I should have started sooner, and Jacques Delamain, my other master, was born too late. What is more, if one wants to know birds, one needs sharp eyes. Only one part of me was a birder and enjoyed the delightful surprises that come with it. I got the robin which would swoop down menacingly at La Chatte's forehead. I took some diversion, one short season, in a multitude of wagtails and the boldness with which they

Flora and Pomona

followed after my gardener; he would throw them grubs and worms dug up by the edge of his spade, and they would snatch them from the air, like domestic chickens. A pair of finches that I stuffed with seed would enter the little dining room by swooping past La Chatte on the sill. If, at the brush of a wing, the forgotten glint of the huntress would light up in La Chatte's eyes, I had only to scold her gently, "Chatte!" and, so as not to displease me, she would extinguish her lamps of perdition . . .

It was my analphabetic gardener—I won't say his name, his wife is still in mourning for him—who taught me to hang nests made of hollowed-out birch logs with a round opening cut into them, when he learned of my predilection for the one Buffon, I think, calls "the fiercest of all birds." He knew nothing of Buffon, but was well acquainted with the titmouse, and he found the name Buffon endlessly funny. He would lean on the handle of his spade to get a good look at one of my favorites, blue as the bluebird, green and yellow as the alder in spring, which right before our eyes rid the tree of caterpillars, scrutinized the bark, and disappeared under a tunnel of dead leaves, only to re-emerge with a full beak and return to her nest, which she entered sometimes head down, sometimes climbing vertically, nimble on her flexible little claws. From her threshold she sent us a comminatory message, a triumphant "turrruititittit," which no doubt demanded our applause for her titmouse prowess, her titmouse labors, her titmouse acrobatics . . . Then my gardener would shake his head and laugh to himself as if remembering an old Marseilles story and

say, "Oh, that Buffon . . . No, my friends, that Buffon!
. . . It'll make me laugh as long as I live . . . !"

In a merger of journalistic reportage and the cinema—
the latter in the form of a screenplay bought from me
by an Italian firm—I had the chance to spend four
months in Rome, from December 1916 to March 1917.
Italian war rationing has, I confess, left memories free
of bitterness: fifteen grams of sugar a day, a knob of
butter, bread measured out in thin slices, and goodness
knows what else . . . Rome was awash in a damp, smoky
winter and I delighted in so much mildness, so much
humidity in the air, in weather at times like Nice in
sunshine; at times rather close and hazy, like the blue
air that sits in a circle on the ground around hot springs.
        An Italian film company acquired the rights to the
screen adaptation of the most well known of my novels
and hired the latest French vamp, whom I nicknamed
Musidora. She brought to Rome her plucky spirit, her
lovely eyes, her long, perfect legs, her striking black
and white beauty destined for the silver screen, which
Italian directors found *troppo italiana*. A simpering *bion-
dinetta* would have been more to their liking. As a
brunette femme fatale, Francesca Bertini was, at the
time, as much as they could handle.
        I'm going back now to a heroic age of cinema,
when flesh-and-blood stars dove and threw themselves
beneath speeding cars, traveled on train axles, and rode
on the backs of runaway horses.
        In Italy, where there is no shortage of architectural
wonders, one would send a young woman of the hum-

blest background to darn her little family's socks and underwear on terraces and balconies that had seen no less than Cesare Borgia pass. In a sitting room, the number of armchairs, indeed the number of pianos, was a sign of ostentation, compensating for a lack of quality.

Since I did not speak the language of the country, I did not make a good visitor to the Eternal City, and was an even worse visitor to its museums, which I would leave feeling crushed and timid, overwhelmed by masterpieces. I fortified myself in rather modest restaurants, and that of the Basilica Ulpia always had something I could content myself with, since it could always provide me with, in addition to a plateful of pasta, a daily mound of small, new artichokes sealed in boiling oil and crisp as fried roses.

The filming was coming along slowly. Rented cars carried the main actors great distances. Musidora, covered in romantic ruffles of pink tulle, wearing a big straw hat tied with a black velvet bow, would romp through the meadows. I never could figure out why. I believe it was because the director was a poet. He proved it to me several days later.

In order to film a small artists' party, with painters and models, he wanted permission to shoot in a prince's garden, bereft of its masters and strictly closed to visitors. One day in April, I went in with him, in spite of a hostile guardian made entirely of boxwood, which held the gate half open and gave us some argument. But already an imperious and formal paradise was rushing to meet us in such a way that it alone would have sufficed to hold our curiosity at bay.

I will not try to describe such a creation, human and vernal, or so considered a use of the season of exuberance. I felt the warmth of a mauve sun on my eyelids as together the transparency and the thickness of a curtain of wistarias changed the color of day without obstructing the quick light. Countless long clusters, on a vertical hidden armature, streamed down to the ground. Another effect, this one of waves and rain, fell from the weeping willows in parallel strands of fine hair. Freer in movement than the wistaria, they veiled and unveiled other green architectures, intercalary bits of sky, blue and violet lawns, a brazier of japonicas, an island of the palest lilacs thinned out against a sky nearly as colorless as themselves, a cloud of double cherry trees of a perfect whiteness, and paulownias and Judas trees, unreal in the distance, like all mauve things . . .

Following the paths of fine sand that did not cry out underfoot, I noticed that they bore no footprints. Some builder of Edens had long ago handed out mass and color. What surprised me was that all still obey him today. A master, long since deceased, continued to direct the garden and its running waters, here turned into serpents in the folds of stone along the footpaths, there into draperies held up against the light so that through them one could glimpse a patch of trembling landscape, a fairyland racked with sobs.

The ornaments of a three-hundred-year-old style were still standing. A long cane of water, spun crystal, was shooting from a satyr's mouth. A nymph's charming backside reposed in the center of a wheel of water.

Flora and Pomona

A shell became a spring, a dolphin a double frond of water . . .

Perhaps there are other gardens in Italy with as many estimable charms, paths where only birds walk, fountains from which no mouth drinks. I saw only that one, and could neither forget it nor fall for it as I can for a dell, a happy farm, or a gatekeeper's lodge ablaze with bitter apple, hollyhocks, and dahlias . . . It owed too much to human will, sure of itself, laying out nature without a single mistake.

Beside me, the director was completely carried away, explaining how such a location seemed ideal for the choreographic frolic. He ran on ahead of me, climbed a crumbling flight of stairs, and hopped down, landing squarely on the flank of a reclining goddess who, from high atop a long, warm, empty terrace, looked out over Rome.

"And over there . . . There," he cried out, inspired, "the line for the cakewalk!"

When there were oranges . . . Ever since we've been without them, the name alone is enough to set flowing, in our deprived mouths, the clear saliva that greets a freshly cut lemon, raw sorrel, or peppery pimpernel. But our need for oranges goes beyond craving. We want to *see* oranges, too. We think of that reflection, that footlight which rose up from heavily laden carts to the faces leaning over them in the street. We want to buy one, two, ten kilos of oranges. We want to feel their weight, to carry off those cut branches, bearers of glossy leaves and mandarins, that blaze the stalls of the Cours Saleya in Nice, all along the flower market. We feel a terrible longing for those round baskets which perfumed our hotel room and which we would send to our friends in Paris (the woman who sold them to us would throw in, beneath the cover, a bunch of violets and a sprig of mimosa) . . . These little memories, bittersweet, exasperating . . . They seem so real that we are left feeling somewhat craven. There were also those tiny local mandarins, puffed out around their equator, which, under your nail, exuded an abundance of essential oil through their pores . . . There was that excellent Italian delicacy made of muscat grapes preserved in syrupy wine, shriveled in the sun, mummified and heady, rolled in vine leaves. There were fruits crystallized with sugar, shot through with sugar, that were nothing but sugar, with all the glossy transparency of semihard stones— topaz-apricots, jade-melons, chalcedony-almonds, ruby-cherries, amethyst-figs . . . One day at Cannes I saw a little boat made of colored sugar overflowing with its cargo of candied fruits. It could easily have held two passengers. What sweet tooth, what spoiled child had embarked his dream aboard such a skiff? I entered . . . "It's been sold, madame." "And for how much?" "Five thousand francs." Five thousand prewar francs, five thousand francs in 1931 . . .

Will I be reproached for bringing up, not without cruelty, a rather painful subject? . . . I protest that for some time now we have been trained to face wartime shortages squarely and unflinchingly. It is a good form of mental exercise. Moreover, many a one who doesn't bat an eye at the sight of a bar of chocolate weakens at the mere thought of a fresh orange still wearing a little leaf on its stem. I confess that I am such a one. An orange . . . but not just any orange. Westerners have yet to be educated. Listen to them ordering in restaurants: "I'll have an orange," as if there were only one kind in all the world, one crop, one tree, one indistinct multitude of oranges . . .

It is February as I write these lines. This is the time when in more peaceful years we used to savor the Tunisians, the elite of orange groves. Oval and a little puffy around the base of its stem, the Tunisian floods the mouth with juice that is never bland, is mildly tart and generously sweetened. Intact, its peel exhales a fragrance reminiscent of the orange blossom itself. December to February is the short season for gorging oneself on Tunisians. As very characteristic vintages differ from bottle to bottle, one Tunisian is never exactly like the next, and the slight difference encourages the opening of another one, and another, and yet another, which may be the best of all . . .

After the Tunisian, I had the Philippeville, which is not its equal but its replacement, is rich and juicy and pleasantly sweet if it has been a sunny year. Then came the Palermitan, just as March and April brought on a growing thirst. With the sun rising in concert with the thermometer, I later would have to resort to oranges from Brazil and Spain. But Spain keeps its best fruit for itself and we wrongly accuse all Spanish oranges of leaving an aftertaste of raw onion.

Last of all, the mad consumption of orangeade brought to both Paris and the beaches a small orange that ripens late on cold Iberian plateaus. It was most welcome, just when the cherries and the strawberries, passing as in a dream, were leaving us.

In the Midi we would buy the ugly summer orange by the hamperful so we could squeeze its pale, meager flesh and spice up its juice by mixing it with the juice of freshly picked lemons. For if the Provençal lemon is worthy of moistening fish and shellfish, the local orange is little more than the ornament of flowery enclosures, the garden's yellow moon, the something extra in a homemade preserve. Extend its credit no further. Instead, praise the second fig, which from the loveliest hours of summer makes its honey, swells with nocturnal dew, and, green and purple, cries through its eye a lone tear of delicious gum, to mark the precise moment of its perfection. Eat it under the tree, and if you value my esteem, never leave it in a cool place, or—horror and sacrilege!—in crushed ice, all-purpose last resort invented by the crude American palate, which paralyzes all flavor, stiffens the melon, anesthetizes the strawberry, and changes a ring of pineapple into fiber more textile than edible.

The fruit room-temperature, the water in the glass cold: that is how water and fruit seem best. What is one to make of a fruit that is removed, like a cooling planet, from the warmth that formed it? An apricot picked and eaten in the sun is sublime. The hour I spent in a Moroccan orange grove is as alive in my memory and in my gratitude as if I still had the yellow line under my nails left there by a glut of the ripest oranges. Dark, smallish, with a cheek sometimes rubbed with bright red rouge, by ten o'clock on an April morning they were already warm, when the tall spring grass at our feet still cooled our ankles. Were one of us to stop as if out of discretion, the Moroccan servant would raise his arm, point toward the horizon, and laugh, to make us understand that farther on, as far as the eye could see, other tangerines awaited us, beyond number . . .

Marrakesh gave us still more. Pure water, roses, nightingales that at a given nocturnal signal would all break into song at once, onrushing dawns that would invade the sky like a conflagration—and oranges on the orange trees of the Pasha Si Hadj Thami el Glaoui. Opulent orange groves of a master at once discriminating and lavish, the secret alignment of what on first approach appears provocatively random, but what pains produced and protected such harvests! Their fragrance, falling from above, trailed across the ground and nearly barred our passage. Waxy petals fell in a steady rain, carrying the drunken bees along with them as they fell; the bees hit the ground with them, got up covered with dust, and found their way back to the blossoms hanging among the fruit. In its turn an orange would fall, a big, heavy, egg-shaped orange that split as it hit the ground and bled a pink blood from its fall . . . Not far off, the pink walls of the city, against a sky already bleached by the heat, enclosed this paradise—and a well-guarded paradise it was. If I raised a hand toward its golden fruit, the sinewy black arm of the Moroccan angel would burst through the leaves, brandishing a stick . . . But one word from our guide and the bronze arm, swallowed back up for a moment, reappeared, its dark palm tendering a juicy orange.

A hot city grafts onto us memories of an earlier time, memories dearer than the plentiful waters that enrich it, reflect its sky, keep its trees green, swell its fruit, and play with its sands. The Aguedal in Marrakesh is a vast and shimmering mirror framed with greenery; none of the reflections I saw tremble in it ever fade. Like a silver nail, many are the fountains that fix the image of a garden I have loved. For how many years did I stop, once each year, at Aix-en-Provence, on the way from Paris to Saint Tropez, because of a spring that has been rushing from a fountain for a thousand years? I would dip my cup in the ancient waters, imitating the spring's devotees, the old woman with her carafe, the boy with his jug, the little brown-haired girl with her umbilicate pitcher. I would drink deeply from the fresh, sweet waters of Aix. The Roman fountain is a link in my desires: every time I saw water in a confined place well up, gurgle, and leap, I wanted to carry it off and plant it in my own garden, even the old fountain of Salon, a mammoth bearded with grass, whose every bristle channels its own drop of water. A garden without a spring does not murmur enough, and my longings have yet to be cut off from the living waters of my childhood, surging up from my native soil in a small flood, no sooner born than lost, known to the shepherd, tramps, hunting dogs, the fox, and the bird. One was in a wood, and autumn covered it with dead leaves; one was in a meadow, beneath the grass and so perfectly

Flora and Pomona

round that a crown of white narcissus, equally round, would give it away, but only in springtime. One flowed like music from the side of the road; one was a pale-blue gem, shimmering in a vat of roughly piled stones, and crawfish swam in its inverted sky. I am assured that the last is still as pure, but that it leaps, with a vain crystal effort, between four cement walls, the gift of human farsightedness; but my taste runs only to untamed springs, watched over by the wide-eyed forget-me-nots and mayflowers and the big salamander spotted like a pied horse.

I wanted a spring in my garden—I want one still, though I no longer have a garden, and the one in the Palais-Royal has had no water since the war began. Jean Giono promised me one quite recently. And as I received his promise around a nicely laid table in celebration of my seventieth birthday, a slight tipsiness sketched the image of a sparkling, glittering spring in the bottom of my glass, and of a Jean Giono, as blond as the wine, source of springs I might carry with me always. "To you I give the loveliest of my springs," he said generously. We shall see. Why change what I have always wished for? Jean Giono's spring may be the most real of all. If these lines reach the man whose domains extend from mountainsides to sheep and waterfalls, he will know that I possess in spirit what he has given me. His spring has joined my varied treasures. Some are tangible, like the glass paperweights in whose centers is a twisted, frozen frenzy of hard crack sugars, flowers, and bacteria; like the oat grains that have feelers like a shrimp's and which, testing the air and turning this way and that, predict good or bad weather; like a glass gem polished by the sea whose color equals aquamarine. "Do you know what this is?" asked one mean friend. "It's the bottom of a seltzer bottle tossed around a while by the waves." Never show skeptics treasures washed up by the sea.

But I have more than movables. I have exclusive possession of nearly everything I have lost—even my dear departed ones. In which regard I resemble a little trout-colored horse I drove one summer long ago. On a road in Picardy, he came across a harrow standing idle during the farmer's siesta. The little trout-colored horse, a Parisian, lost his composure so utterly, wheeling around, shying back, lowering his head between his forelegs, arching his back like a mermaid, that nothing could prevail upon him or reassure him and we could get home only by taking the long way back. Then he and I both forgot about the harrow; until one day when, on the same road, at the same spot, the little trout-colored horse suddenly stopped stone still—any more suddenly and I would have tumbled over the edge of the cart.

"What's the matter?" I asked him.

"There . . ." said the little horse, trembling. "There . . . !"

"There what? A grass snake?"

"No . . . The monster . . . The same one . . ."

On the empty road, he could see the ghost of the harrow so clearly that the next moment he broke into a sweat. His muscular nostrils flared and he could not tear his gaze from the phantom harrow, from the image of a triangular bogey etched in his big ink-blue eyes.

Fright aside, I often have been that visionary little

horse. Life is hard pressed to dispossess me. I shall never stop going over what chance once made mine. I am still at it, while my oldest friend, Léon Barthou, has preferred the unintelligible repose of the dead to the quiet company of his books, his favorite armchair, and his cat; I am still at it as I gaze past his brown Béarnaise face to the celestial horizon, the small, flat earth one discovers from high up in a free balloon, and I inventory the instruments thrown pell-mell into the giant picnic basket that is a lighter-than-air craft . . .

"Léon, what do you call the gadget that hung above your head, from your spherical balloon, that thingamajig that looked like an overgrown earthworm you'd grab hold of every now and then?"

I question him still; nothing has changed, except that he no longer answers. I still fly over Versailles with him, at low altitude, over the mosaics and mirrors of its park; a gust of wind carries us back over Paris, and the shadow of the net's mesh revolves on the underbelly of the sphere . . . Enclosed gardens everywhere in the city . . . The pearly sound of the ballast tossed into the Seine rises up to us, and our sudden, imperceptible surge steals from us the imprisoned gardens, all of which contain a bit of dark greenery, a disk that is a table, and another, smaller disk, a child's hat . . .

"Léon, in what street was that garden you pointed out to me, so well tended, so full of flowers, that from up there looked like a tapestry cushion?"

He will answer no more. Besides, so many streets, so many quarters, so many gardens are gone or unrecognizable . . . I change memory-sights, I herborize at random.

And not always in vain. By poring over an image in memory, I sometimes succeed in re-creating a flower that intrigued me in the past. Thus do we call the word back from the abyss, even as it is being swallowed up, which we seize by a syllable, by its first letter, which we raise toward the light, dripping with mortal obscurity . . . I was looking for that tubular calix, its lacy corolla, its cherry color, its name . . . I've got it. I shall never let go of it again, unless it is for good. It is called by the strange name of pentstemon. Having come back to me tamed, as it were, the pentstemon plays its part quite nicely in an orchestration of violet, red, and mauve which the city gardener conducts as best he can—red and pink gladiolus, red and pink dahlias, the last roses, pink and purple altheas, fiery geraniums, the woolly ageratum, which wavers between blue and lilac, and the pentstemon—enough to last until November, if the autumn is mild.

How many imprisoned Paris gardens have divulged their secrets to me? I would never steal a flower; only rarely have I stolen fruit. But my love of walled gardens is shameless. It was not so long ago that the wrecking crews drove me from a large building, one side of which gave onto the Faubourg Saint-Honoré. Past the second courtyard, through a break in the wall, I had spied an old garden, three stone steps, a bit of grass, and some privet, whose meager flowers strained toward the light.

To what surprise shall I compare the discovery I made, in the sixteenth arrondissement, of a Directoire peristyle around which ran rows of apple trees? Was there fruit on them? It was already too much to hope that they would shed a single petal, like a lost wing, onto the cobblestones of Paris . . . At the end of the rue Jean-Bologne, to the left, I owned, by sheer number of visits, one wall of a provincial-style house, facing south, what was left of a flagstone terrace, and strips of vegetables . . . Rue des Perchamps, three thousand meters of uncultivated garden, hazelnut trees, wild rosebushes, and lime trees for a long time were my lot, thanks to their owner, with whom I had a friendship of some years' standing. On even-numbered days she would want to sell her land. On odd-numbered days she would take it back, saying with an air of finality, "Sell my land in Auteuil? I'm not that stupid!" This went on for years. One even-numbered day, she signed a private agreement and I lost the grounds where I used to go to pick red-skinned filberts and degenerate roses.

Jacques-Emile Blanche gladly offered me his, though I never took him up on it, for fear of spoiling it. It is only now that I stroll there in my mind, since its masters no longer exist, nor the coffee-colored poodle, sensitive, proud of its pedigree, which would cover its forehead with ashes, want to die, to take holy orders, if Jacques-Emile said to him in a low tone of rebuke, "Good gracious, but don't you look common, Puck . . ."

Blanche's garden, with northern exposure like the painter's studio, possessed several of those beautiful trees scattered throughout Passy and Auteuil, which, it was agreed, had known the Princess de Lamballe. In their shade there meandered, for me to admire, a stream painted in particularly blue forget-me-nots, compact and even, hemmed in between two banks of pinks. The blue stream guided visitors to the studio where I posed for three successive portraits. Jacques-Emile Blanche destroyed the first two; the third is in the museum in Barcelona.

During the sittings, the cold light from a large skylight and my fixed position overwhelmed me with drowsiness, and to keep myself awake I would look at two equally ambiguous paintings above my head: the deliciously small Manfred, dressed as a cherub, and Marcel Proust, about eighteen years old, with his thin lips, his big, deep-set eyes, wearing a wholly Oriental expressionlessness. That Jacques-Emile Blanche should paint anything other than a Jacques-Emile Blanche is without parallel. Only the portrait of Marcel Proust differs from the rest of his work, through an extraordinarily sleek handling, a fondness for symmetry, the exaltation of a real and short-lived beauty. Illness, work, and talent refashioned that smooth face, and those soft cheeks, pale and Persian, and disheveled the hair, which was not in the least silken or fine, but coarse, with a frightening vitality, thick as the blue-black beard that was no sooner shaved than it pierced the skin . . . Those who spent evenings with Marcel Proust recall seeing his beard darken between ten at night and three in the morning, at the same time that, under the influence of fatigue and alcohol, the very character of his physiognomy would change.

I remember a dinner at the Ritz, begun quite late and drawn out into supper and talk. At the time, Marcel Proust was still in his better days, a charming and almost young man, brimming with excess of kindness, with a beseeching thoughtfulness painted in his gaze. But toward four in the morning I had before me a sort of best man under the influence, his white cravat in need of straightening, his chin and cheeks blackened with fresh growth, a big lock of dark hair fanned out between his eyebrows . . . "Oh, that's not him . . ." whispered one guest. Quite to the contrary, I was waiting for the appearance of the sinner, ravaged but powerful, who by the weight of his genius would stagger the frail young man in tails . . .

That moment never came. Night turned into dawn and paled only under cover of the most seductive small talk. No one is better guarded than the one who appears to give himself up to any and all. Behind his first line of defense breached by the brandy, Marcel Proust, reaching positions deeper and more difficult to break through, was watching us.

When Francis Jammes, in a preface that greatly honored the first book signed with my name, credited me with having *La Maison rustique des Dames* as my bedside book, he was anticipating. I was busy then with various forms of cultivation, but without the authoritative guide mentioned by the poet, and led only by a whimsical spirit with the limitations of youth. It is only now that Francis Jammes is closest to the truth. Alongside my *Grande Pomologie*, the *Trochilidés* of Lesson, the *Roses* signed Redouté, the *Herbier de l'amateur* by Lemaire, and several remarkable and incomplete botanical tomes, Mme Millet-Robinet and her homespun wisdom about housekeeping, grafting, cooking, and planting are always at hand.

I abide, unblushingly, by the advances in farming and homemaking made in the last century. Apart from the uses to which electricity and machinery have been put, I would do just fine were I still the proprietor of a few acres in the country. As it happens, after various vicissitudes, everything I own once again fits into a drawer and on bookshelves. Raising rabbits in the cellar, chickens in the attic, or a heifer in the passages beneath the Palais-Royal is out of the question. At the risk of finding my reputation ruined, I have never fed a single creature I might have had to eat, not even one of those pigeons that never live up to their billing, for the bird of Venus is in truth callous and quarrelsome, with cruel, red-gold eyes, and as for the female pigeon's legendary fidelity—on that score, it is better that my reader keep his illusions.

I have seen my mother call the chickens in our poultry yard, and the chicks peck at the crumbs and feed from her hands; and the warm, pink eggs go from nest to table, and the chicks clamber into our laps. In my memory an anguished cry marks the end of the hen house. "Oh, my God . . . kill the little red hen?" wept my mother. Whereafter the poultry yard was left deserted, the cats slept in the wicker coops, we ate none but strange chickens, and the two hen houses became storerooms where the corms of the dahlias and the bulbs of the hyacinths, the tulips, and the crocuses slept in winter . . . Still, Sido, my mother, lamented her inability to be a vegetarian. "I can't eat lentils because they look like lice," she would say. "I don't eat Chinese artichokes because they have the same vague shape as cockchafer grubs, and I don't like broad beans because they taste of swamp. Peas? If I don't pick them myself, they don't get picked until they've turned to buckshot. Cauliflower is a disgrace to the house while it's cooking . . . That leaves butter, eggs, and fruit. Speaking of which, Mme Millet-Robinet says . . ."

I did not listen to the gospel according to Mme Millet-Robinet. But I have since made amends, be it only learning and relearning from her forgotten names and the code of a simple country life, new for having been forsaken, and somehow younger, so much have we, by growing away from it, grown old ourselves.

More has been lost than the bonhomie of an earlier existence. Its diversity, which we lack, came from a good many objects and the uses to which they were put. Neither those objects nor their uses appealed to what we have come to call selection, an evil that comes to us from America, with its two apples, the red and the yellow, the red and its hardy crimson, its healthy tastelessness, like that of raw vegetables—the yellow and its tart juice, a bit more individual. Right away the fruit specialist wants to "select," and to discuss size, shipping, and preservation. Calvilles, pippins from Canada, pippins and Calvilles: there was no getting out from under them, if you don't count a few truckloads of cooking apples. When we see pears again, will Paris once more settle for the Duchesse and the Passecrassane, with a brief interlude of Beurrée Hardy and the rare comice for the lucky few? The nineteenth century benefited more from our riches. Oh, charming end of the nineteenth century, with what grace you savored, squandered, compared . . . I picked up your trail, your squire's taste for the country, your quickness to emerge from anonymity, in short your signature throughout a humble domain, which was mine five or six years after belonging for many years to an elderly gentleman. Those ten hectares, untended since his death, still showed signs of proprietorial primping, of just the sort of planting know-how I like. If I let myself go and conjure them up, I shall fall to moaning and groaning and leading the mourning over twelve hundred fruit trees, already quite old when I got them, their variety the result of caprice no less than sound judgment. Arise, O shades of my pear trees! Who sings, who sows, who knows Messire Jean's pears? Who knows that beneath its reddish-brown jacket, in a shape neighboring on spherical, there hides crisp, juicy flesh and flavor heightened by a pleasant, characteristic tartness? Mme Millet-Robinet gives the gray Messire Jeans their just deserts, and so do I, but who will restore them to favor with the masses?

At the tips of the bare branches, the harsh wind of the Franche-Comté would rock my thin-stemmed gray pears. Below the sparsely leaved, scaly Messire Jean trees exposed to the wind, other early pears would begin to ripen in July, quickly turning mealy if not picked on time, and craftily emptied out by the wasps. They would bore a single hole in the pears, then busy themselves inside while the fruit retained its shape. How many times have I crushed a yellow, wasp-filled Montgolfier in my hand? I can still see the Cuisse Madame, as shapely as its name, and I shall never forget the apples chosen from among the varieties Mme Millet-Robinet names as "obedient to the cordon" . . . With the Doux d'Argent, the short-start, and the Belle-Fleur, I was provisioned with apples year round, as well as plums, although the trees of the greengage, the yellow "monsieurs," and the "purple damson" were weakened and wept gummy tears. Countless daughters of the Comté, one cheek freckled, the other green as amber, the mirabelles, friends of the Doubs, would rain down on the heads of the cats, and the dog would gobble up the best ones.

There were such red, such royal harvests of cherries in July that they would dry up on the ground, shriveled but edible. "Even the blackbirds don't want them," my neighbor assured me. "We'll make a little homemade kirsch out of them . . ." He said this the way they used to say it, in a tone of slightly contemptuous complacency that scoffed at ease and plenty. How easily our hands filled with such riches . . . Such goodness for the taking, always there to make up for lean years . . . The service and the sorb trees in the woods, the cornel-berry trees hanging over the walls of the poultry yard so that the chickens might peck at the cornel berries—or dog-berries—which stain the earth red; the quince trees relegated to the role of quicksets, side by side with the hog plum, the hook apple, the spiny wild currant, mulberries, the downy small peach—all fruits and berries without owners, fallen from the hand of God into the hand of the passerby . . . When gathered, off they went, helter-skelter, into the cask where the marc brandy would gather its sneaky strength and its pithy savor.

I had no intention of reviving the fruit trees on the ten hectares placed in my care by topping and boldly grafting them, even though the mysterious art of grafting leaves most gardeners' heads spinning. The scion, spliced and left to rest and soften in a damp, dark place, then inserted into the slit in the wild or worn-out subject, then dressed with grafting wax, its stump bandaged with cloth and raffia, then adopted by the tree it revives —I can assure the uninformed that a proud pounding of the heart greets the moment when the dormant bud of the scion, which had been sleeping on the foreign stem, wakes, turns green, asserts its paradoxical nature, and enjoins the eglantine with its rose, the plum tree with its peach, its nectarine.

The man who would come and do the grafting always carried a grafting knife with him; it had a short and sweet little ivory blade, almond-shaped, accustomed to stripping the bark without wounding the willows, taking care around the "eyes." For those grafts that were delicate, he would suck on the blade, bestowing human saliva with restorative powers, and say, "Having a good hand isn't everything; when it comes to grafting, you've gotta think . . ." So it is that prayer, in the form of conjuring, slips in everywhere . . .

Propagation by cuttings is less thrilling than graftage and involves no magic. And yet I never became complacent about the moment in my garden when the cutting that has lost consciousness and seems to be succumbing to the brutal incision decides to live, reopens its green canals to the rising sap, and draws itself up with little, imperceptible twitches . . .

In Provence, between one rising and one setting of the sun, I planted seven hundred slips of pink ivy geranium. The only help I received came from the woman who was my gardener. It is one task that can be accomplished sitting down, comfortably set up, right on the loose ground, with the dibble dexter, while advancing the way legless cripples do. The following year the result was lovely. But there is less pleasure to be had in filling out a vast uniform tapestry than in the variation of a many-colored embroidery. If I pay more mind to the shoots, bulbs, coronas, and runners of the Franche-Comté, it is because I was a witness to their exertions and good will, for on that hillside in the Comté, I braved blustery Easters as well as bitter-cold Novembers. If you want to link yourself to a region, don't talk to me so much about the nice times of year as about the bad! A peasant saying goes, "There's no better cure for an ill than the four seasons." Perhaps what I lacked, before I could form solid ties to the lovely Midi, were its unsettled between-seasons: autumn with its lashing rains, which gut the hillsides and wash away the topsoil; the precocious, moody spring, which freezes the thin-walled houses, traps the smoke, and carts off in its squalls almond tree petals, hailstones, and mimosa balls.

A harsh climate that held no surprises watched over my patch of earth in the Franche-Comté. Won over by its hearty welcome and its severity alike, I never disfigured the quenouille-trained pear trees; I merely trimmed, ever so slightly, the hundred-year-old species. There were astonishing acacias hollowed out like smokestacks, from which in dry weather there rained down a dusting of charred wood, like coffee grounds; the melodious larches, the black firs, the silvery limes that summer surrounds with perfume and bees. The monkey puzzle went on gesticulating with all its simian arms. Why should I, just passing through, have infringed upon a decor already a bit too uneven, too fiddled with, but well established in the layout of its paths, groves, rockeries, and views. A man who patiently, ingeniously torments his parcel of land, at the same time he brings to it the productive man's open, hardworking bent of mind, invests it with what we later call a style. Style is nearly always the bad taste of our predecessors, dating from the day we find it to our liking. Besides, short of destroying it, the style of a restricted landscape cannot be shoved about like common cottage furniture. What am I saying? It is the enclosed garden, the landscape laid out by the old gentleman, born before 1830, whose footsteps I follow into the house, which I enter, if I may say so, hard on his heels. He brought an oval drop-leaf table made of black pear wood, at which I ate and wrote, around which there came to be grouped other pieces of furniture neither old nor rare; but I was perfectly content with them. I can think of nothing more to say about them, unless it is that the exceptional piece—the "find," as they say—often causes a big fuss and commotion in a quiet interior and leaves it bewildered. No, I shall not describe any further what was peaceful, a bit drab, a bit heavy, good by the corner of the fire in winter, and in summer at the edge of a lovely, bellied stoop.

Just understand that a person of my sort, led blindfolded into the house, might have predicted that around the dwelling a garden would fill itself out so that pride of place—honor where honor is due—went to the wig sumac: that bourgeois miracle, a spiderweb for nocturnal dew, a snare for jewels of rain and rainbows, the tree with vaguely pink pompons like clouds; in short, the *Rhus cotinus*, do you know the one? No, not any longer.

Rhus cotinus, angel's wig, your ineluctable presence guaranteed us the ornamental currant bush with yellow clusters and the sterile black-currant bush with pink flowers. When, in an amateur's garden, *Rhus cotinus* and fruitless currant bushes took their place in the front rank, who would have supplanted the bladdernut tree behind them, filled with the tintinnabulation of vesicular pods and the violaceous althea? What innovator would have taken it upon himself to bar the way to the *Fritillaria* known as crown imperial, to its orange-colored flower heads, to its smell of bad company? The subjects she gathered around her were pink and white pyrethrums, Corylopsis, and winter cherries veined like lungs, and an abundance of flowers for borders, white and faint-smelling, which were called Thlaspi or theraspic, depending on the region. If the border Thlaspi failed, it would be replaced by a plant that resembled, feature for feature, the shaggy ear of a white donkey. For along the edge of a flower bed, and all around a massed group of flowers, there had to be a border, a verge, and along that border another border of little rounded tiles, and sometimes the shell-shaped tile was protected by an overborder of wire wickets.

All this comes back to me as I write, all this that flowered long ago, those curves, that softness of design, the primness and the habits of a traditional way of gardening—all this banished by another tradition embraced by cement and flagstones repointed with grass, bronze cypress trees, atriums, pergolas, and patios . . . Still, a slightly Irish straightforwardness strews the undergrowth of the woods with daffodils, saffron crocuses, and snowflakes, and credits the garden with wild Labiatae and Aaron's-rod . . .

What would Mme Millet-Robinet have said about such oft-imitated laxity? She foresaw it, since, from high up in her *Maison rustique*, from the threshold of her proper floriculture, she says, "In a well-cultivated garden everything must bear the stamp of order. All flower beds must be round." Sido put it more simply: "I don't want weeds anywhere but on my grave." In matters of gardening, my two oracles are thus in agreement over banishing what is easy, and all I need do is follow them, Mme Millet-Robinet out of deference, Sido out of love, if . . .

. . . If I had a garden. Now, as it so happens, I no longer have a garden. It isn't so terrible not to have a garden. It would be serious if the future garden, whose reality matters little, were beyond my grasp. It is not. A certain crackling of seeds in their paper packets is all it takes to sow the air. A seed of love-in-a-mist is black, brilliant as a hundred fleas, and, if heated, will smell of apricots for a long time, a quality it does not pass on to its flower. I shall sow love-in-a-mist when, in the garden of tomorrow, dreams, plans, and recollection have taken, have taken hold in the form of what I once owned and of what I am now banking on. To be sure, the hepaticas there will be blue, for the winy pink ones try my patience. Blue, and in sufficient numbers to edge the circular flower bed ("All flower beds must be round . . .") that raises Dielytras to become *pendeloques*, weigelas, and double deutzias. The only pansies I shall have are those that look like Henry VIII—broad-faced, bearded, and mustachioed; some saxifrage only if, one fine summer evening, when I politely offer them a lighted match, they respond with their harmless little burst of gas . . .

An arbor? Of course I shall have an arbor! I still have an arbor or two in me. The dragon-tongued, violet cobaea, the Polygonum, and the oar-driven melon must have a trellis perch . . . "Oar-driven melon"? Why not "motor-driven squash"? Because the melon I am talking about paddles and plies its way up any support just like a simple pea, leaving in its wake little green-and-white melons, sweet and bursting with flavor. (See the writings of Mme Millet-Robinet.)

If the lovers of horticultural novelties were to banish all the old love-lies-bleeding, I of course would take several in, if only to give them back their old name: nuns' disciplines. They will get on well with the feathery pampas grass, a decent sort, not too smart, who spends the winter on either side of the fireplace in cone-shaped vases.

Come summer, we will jilt the pampas grass and in its vases plant the suffocating white lily, more imperious than orange blossoms, more passionate than the tuberose; lilies that ascend the stair at midnight and seek us out in our deepest sleep.

If it is a garden in Brittany—how I love my ideal parterre plumed with pointed "ifs"—daphne . . . Must we call it daphne, or "*bois gentil*," this small, concealed flower, immense by virtue of its fresh, noble scent, which breaks on the Breton winter air as early as January? In the showers that come with the tide from the west, a bush of "*bois gentil*" seems doused with perfumes. If I plant myself at the edge of a lake, I shall have, besides the dense shrubbery the deceased Old Gentleman used to train, I shall have Chimonanthus in winter, in daphne's stead. The Chimonanthus, a December flower, has all the color and brightness of a cork shaving. It has one distinction, which is sure to give it away. In one place in Limousin, where I was unaware of its presence, in snowy weather I sensed, sought, and found it in the icy air, guided by its fragrance. On its branch it is dingy and dull, but gifted with great powers of seduction—when I think of Chimonanthus I think of nightingales. So, I shall have Chimonanthus . . . Don't I already?

I shall have many others, verbena rosettes, Aristolochia pipes, thrift tufts, Maltese cross crosses, lupine spikes, and moonflower insomniacs, Agrostis nebulae, and vanilla pinks, St.-John's-cane to help me along the final steps I travel, and asters to star my nights. A Campanula, a thousand Campanulas, to ring in the dawn at the same time the cock crows; a dahlia gadrooned like a Clouet strawberry; a digitalis so that the fox will have gloves—or so claims its common name; a Julienne, and not, as you might think, diced into the soup, but as a border! A border, I'm telling you, a border. Lobelias as a border, too, whose blue neither sky nor sea can rival. As for honeysuckle, I'll pick the most frail, which grows weak and wan for being so odoriferous . . . Last of all,

I must have a magnolia that is a good layer, all covered with its white eggs as Easter approaches; a wistaria that, abandoning its long flowers drop by drop, turns the terrace into a purple lake. And lady's-slippers, enough to shoe the whole house. Don't offer me any rose laurel, I want only roses and laurel.

My choice does not mean that, once assembled, the flowers I have named will please the eye. And besides, I've forgotten some. But there's no rush. I am heeling them in, some in my memory, others in my imagination. Where, by the grace of God, they still find the rich soil, the slightly bitter waters, the warmth and the gratitude that will perhaps keep them from dying.

SOURCES

For an Herbarium

Pour un Herbier. Lausanne: Mermod, 1948. pp. 9–123.

A Nosegay
   From the Midi

Belles Saisons. Paris: Flammarion, 1955. pp. 7–9.

   Snowdrop

Mélanges, Oeuvres Complètes, XV. Paris: Le Fleuron, 1949–50. pp. 339–340.

Flower Shows

Aventures Quotidiennes. Paris: Flammarion, 1924. pp. 65–73.

Flora and Fauna of
   Paris and Environs

Paysages et Portraits. Paris: Flammarion, 1958. pp. 114–119.

December in the Fields

Paysages et Portraits. Paris: Flammarion, 1958. pp. 119–121.

Secrets	*Prisons et Paradis*. Paris: Ferenczi, 1932. pp. 165–171.
Redouté's Roses	*Mélanges*. Oeuvres Complètes, XV. Paris: Le Fleuron, 1949–50. pp. 235–339.
The Life and Death of the Phyllocactus	*Paysages et Portraits*. Paris: Flammarion, 1958. pp. 265–267
Flora and Pomona	*Flore et Pomone*. Paris: Editions de la Galérie Charpentier, 1943. Reprinted in *Gigi*. Paris: Ferenczi, 1945. pp. 137–182.